My Story

The Act of Storytelling

Richard J. Bishirjian, Ph.D.

En Route Books and Media, LLC
Saint Louis, MO

ENROUTE
Make the time

En Route Books and Media, LLC
5705 Rhodes Avenue
St. Louis, MO 63109

Contact us at **contactus@enroutebooksandmedia.com**

Cover Credit: Avery Easter

ISBN-13: 979-8-88870-359-5
Library of Congress Control Number: 2025936115

Table of Contents

Part One

"Among the many complaints about the modern American novelist, the loudest, if not the most intelligent, has been the charge that he is not speaking for his country."[1]

Flannery O'Connor's observation above does not apply to the political theorist whose first obligation is to his country. That explains why ***My Story***, though intensely personal, is enwrapped in concern for the United States.

Nations, and individual men and women, have histories which they express in the form of "Stories." Each is different, and some are more important than others. The Book of Mathew in the New Testament traces the line of Jesus from Abraham through David. How that "Story" of Jesus waxed and waned over the centuries defines historical "eras" of the West, the truths shared, and the fates of national communities.

My Story is important because, in writing it, I explain my motives in choosing to become a political philosopher and how thankful I am for the friendship of a few good men, now deceased, for whom I pray to God that He comforts their souls and that He tells them that, in a few years, I will join them. These daily prayers include thanks for the gifts He has showered upon me, including a long life,

---

[1] Flannery O'Connor, "The Regional Writer." In *Mystery and Manners: Occasional Prose* (New York: Farrar, Straus and Cudahy, 1961), 51.

good health, my family and friends, an excellent education, and His Holy Church.

Ancient Rome shaped the form (*eidos*) of civilization in which ***My Story*** is told. That form includes a consciousness of freedom—under Roman law—as valuable. The laws of Rome supported "order" and the lives of Roman citizens. That enabled the protected status of Roman citizenship to St. Paul and freedom to spread the "good news" of Jesus' birth, life, death, and resurrection.

Ancient Kings were long gone by the time ***My Story*** was lived in the 20th Century, but periodizing history as we know it has been a constant since the ancient Greek poet, Hesiod, divided human history into a Golden, Silver, Bronze, and Heroic Age in the 8th–7th century BC. In the ancient world, entire peoples sought relief in the Roman Empire, just as the nations of the West collectively defended themselves against a USSR enlivened by a formidable ideology that fortuitously died in 1991.

The story of the spreading of the good news of Christ Jesus by the Gospel evangelists and Paul of Tarsus continues to shape us even today. That is the context of *My Story*, the grandson, on one side, of Armenian Christians who fled persecution in Turkey and, on the other, of Lutherans who emigrated to the United States from Germany before WW I.

During World War II, my father, Jack Albert Bishirjian, a first-generation American, served with the U.S. Marine Corps in the Pacific Theater on Saipan and Iwo Jima. For him and his fellow Marines—and for me—the United States is the best country in the world. It enabled him, through his "GI Bill," to buy a small building at 3887 Bigelow Boulevard in Pittsburgh, Pennsylvania. There, he sold oriental rugs and later broadloom carpets.

We lived in a small apartment—above the rug store—which included a bedroom where my parents slept, a small "living room," a "sun porch" converted into a bedroom for me, and a small kitchen next to a dinette that my father added after a few years.

As a child, I would carry cups of coffee down the stairs from our apartment to my father and would go on deliveries of rugs to customers who lived in beautiful homes in Oakland and Fox Chapel. The owner of one explained that his home had a hidden room that once served as a refuge for African slaves fleeing their Southern "enslavers." On another occasion, I so energetically displayed small carpets to one customer that she rebuked me for being too pushy. That lady was Elsie Hillman, the wife of a billionaire industrialist.[2]

Though I understood that wealthy Americans lived lives that were quite different from my own, if ever I had any doubts, I needed only to look down from my bedroom window, where I could see a "Timken" retail store on Baum Boulevard, a heavily traveled commercial road.

In addition to selling oriental rugs on consignment from the New York rug market by friends of my grandfather, Hagop "Harry" Bishirjian, my father cleaned oriental rugs in the basement of his oriental rug store. Two vats of soapy liquid provided an opportunity for me and visiting male cousins to become very clean by stripping naked and jumping into those vats of soap.

---

[2] https://en.wikipedia.org/wiki/Elsie_Hillman

There were three or four families on the Boulevard, including us. They included Fr. Golub, an elderly Armenian priest who, lacking a parish, aimlessly walked up and down the boulevard; Roy McHugh, a sportswriter; and Carl and Helen Rosenfeld, whose son, Charles, became a distinguished academic. Bigelow Boulevard was a commercial avenue, not a place you would expect to grow serious writers. Still, both Charles and I earned Ph.D. degrees, he in Geology and I in Politics, and Roy McHugh was a celebrated chronicler of American sports.

For eight years, I walked the two miles from our apartment above "Bishirjian's Oriental Rug Agency" down Bigelow, passed the Royal York Apartments, and continued down to Center Avenue, where I turned onto Neville Street in Oakland and entered my Missouri Synod Lutheran parish school at First Trinity.[3] In 1951, a movie, *Angels in the Outfield*[4] with Paul Douglas and Janet Leigh, was filmed at Forbes Field, the home of the Pittsburgh Pirates, near where I walked those years.

In 5th or 6th grade, I used my bicycle to speed past the Royal York Apartments and down to my parish school, and after school, I walked laboriously back home, pushing my bike uphill until I reached Bigelow, where I remounted and sped home to the rug store. These years, around age 12 or 13, I would catch Major League baseballs hit over the Forbes Field fence during batting practice, and when I was a little older, I would sell the Pittsburgh Post-Gazette during the games.[5] inside the ballpark.

---

[3] https://www.firsttrinity.net/

[4] https://en.wikipedia.org/wiki/Angels_in_the_Outfield_(1951_film)

[5] https://www.post-gazette.com/

On other days, I would ice skate at Duquesne Gardens,[6] a professional ice skating rink where the Pittsburgh Hornets (now the Penguins) played professional hockey and where members of the "Ice Capades" practiced.

Bigelow Boulevard was also the HQ of John H. Harris,[7] who managed the "Ice Capades," and where once I saw Rosey Roswell,[8] the Pirates game announcer, and the Norwegian figure skater, Sonia Henie,[9] who parked her Jaguar roadster at Mr. Harris's front door.

Though my Dad indulged in work, he made himself loved by throwing coins on the floor for me to pick up, ten dollars or more after poker games. Most influential on me, however, was my Missouri Synod Lutheran church and parish school ("East End Lutheran"), which gave my life purpose.

I suspect that my lifelong German Lutheran devotion shielded me from much temptation and any ill effects of my father's post-World War II drinking of "*Seagram's 7,*" which transformed him into an "angry drunk." The absence of his own father's influence—a price that many immigrant families paid as they adjusted to new lives in America—caused him to be absent from much of My Story.

In 1958, at 40, my father sold what had become a successful rug and carpet business to a Syrian-Christian merchant, and we moved from "above the store" to North Miami, Florida.

---

[6] https://en.wikipedia.org/wiki/Duquesne_Gardens

[7] https://en.wikipedia.org/wiki/John_H._Harris_(entertainment)

[8] https://en.wikipedia.org/wiki/Rosey_Rowswell

[9] https://en.wikipedia.org/wiki/Sonja_Henie

I remember my mother explaining that once we moved, I would no longer see my friends in Pittsburgh, but I was excited to leave Pittsburgh for Miami and asked only, "When do we leave?"

My father did not plan, so we stayed with my grandfather, Harry Bishirjian, in North Miami for some time. Later, we moved into the first of two houses that my father built across from the Thunderbird Motel. In 1950, that area was known as "Motel Row," but it is now called "Sunny Isles."

Because we lived on Miami Beach, I was eligible to seek admission to Miami Beach High School. Still, North Miami High School on the Florida mainland was closer, so that was where, at age seventeen, I discovered that I was a good high school debater and public speaker.

I came to love Miami, which I got to know well by riding a Lambretta motor scooter all over from our home on Motel Row. Back then, helmets were not mandatory, and I had some "close calls." I remember that after dark, when returning home from the Mainland, the highway was covered by land crabs,[10] which made the road slippery when crushed by traffic. On another occasion, I was riding close enough to pass a flatbed truck loaded with pipes. I waited instead of passing, and those pipes rolled off onto the road.

At North Miami High, I also came to appreciate my Jewish classmates, especially Stanley Ringler, who became a Reform Rabbi, and two very talented Jewish students from Miami Beach High, Keith

---

[10] https://en.wikipedia.org/wiki/Terrestrial_crab

Barish[11] and Neil Sonnett.[12] In 1958, Stanley Ringler and I attended "Florida Boys' State." We also participated in high school National Forensic League debates and Knights of Pythias oratory contests.

During the annual meeting of the Teamsters, a classmate much bolder than I sought an interview with Jimmy Hoffa[13] at the Fontainebleau Hotel. I remember being invited into Hoffa's suite at the Fontainebleau by an attractive blond female and heard Hoffa curse David Dubinsky, leader of the Ladies Garment Workers Union. Hoffa spent fifteen minutes answering the questions of two high school students, and for that we were celebrated by our classmates for getting a meeting with the Teamster leader.

When it was time to choose a college, instead of the University of Miami or Florida State, I sought admission in 1960 to the University of Pittsburgh and lived for a time with my Uncle Charles Bishirjian and his wife Katherine in Regent Square, a suburb of Pittsburg bordering Schenley Park.[14]

The year 1960 was a Presidential election year, and that contributed to my early interest in seeking elective office in Pennsylvania as a Republican. While at Pitt, however, political ideas became more important for me than seeking elective office when I encountered

---

[11] https://en.wikipedia.org/wiki/Keith_Barish

[12] https://www.abajournal.com/web/article/celebrated-criminal-defense-attorney-neal-sonnett-dies-at-81

[13] https://en.wikipedia.org/wiki/Jimmy_Hoffa

[14] https://bishirjian.substack.com/p/mary-schenley?utm_source=publication-search

representatives of what Russell Kirk called *The Conservative Mind* and met William "Bill" F. Buckley.[15]

Had Richard Nixon won the 1960 election, "My Story" might have been different. But Nixon lost to John F. Kennedy, a Catholic Democrat from Massachusetts. Consequently, I and thousands of conservative Republicans experienced the difficult burden that comes with electoral defeat.

It took another twenty years before we "political conservatives" elected one of our own as President of the United States.

Upon graduation from Pitt in 1964, with no interest in a government job in LBJ's Democrat government, and no interest in selling oriental rugs, I wrote to Fr. Stanley Parry, CSC,[16] chairman of the Government and International Studies Department at the University of Notre Dame and was admitted in January 1965 to graduate studies in Government. That turned out to be Providential. Accompanying my application was a copy of an essay on "Conservatism" that was published in Pitt's literary journal, *Ideas and Figures.*

I had worked on the 1964 Goldwater campaign as chairman of "Pennsylvania Youth for Goldwater-Miller," and my later career was advanced by support from Paul Weyrich, founder of the Free Congress Foundation,[17] and Morton Blackwell, founder of The Leadership Institute.[18] Both were alumni from that campaign, and they

---

[15] https://en.wikipedia.org/wiki/William_F._Buckley_Jr.

[16] https://studylib.net/doc/7599919/stanley-parry--teacher-and-prophet

[17] https://en.wikipedia.org/wiki/Free_Congress_Research_and_Education_Foundation

[18] https://en.wikipedia.org/wiki/Leadership_Institute

shared with me the donor base of their organizations when I needed funds to finance the creation of Yorktown University.

Two colleagues in graduate school at Notre Dame, Angelo Codevilla[19] and Howard Segermark,[20] also alumni from the Goldwater campaign, were supportive. I distinctly recall that Angelo Codevilla called my attention to the Immigration and Nationality Act of 1965,[21] which had been sponsored by New York Cong. Emmanuel Celler and Michigan Sen. Phil Hart, to expand immigration to overcome the influence of citizens of East, Central, and Western Europe who had experienced the threat of Soviet domination and were inclined to vote Republican. I said to Codevilla, "Angelo, we lost more than the 1964 election."

I was fortunate to be studying under Fr. Stanley Parry, CSC (a former student of Willmoore Kendall[22] at Yale graduate school) who was known for his espousal of ideas supportive of traditional order.

That was what I wanted to learn!

Notre Dame was an odd place for a Missouri Synod Lutheran, but I sought a reprieve from "Liberal ideology" that had dominated my studies in political science at Pitt.

If ever I believed in Divine Providence, my choice of graduate studies at Notre Dame was "Providential." All that I am as a scholar may be traced to my studies with five Notre Dame teachers: Fr.

---

[19] https://www.nytimes.com/2021/10/03/obituaries/angelo-codevilla-dead.html

[20] https://heartland.org/about-us/who-we-are/howard-segermark/

[21] https://en.wikipedia.org/wiki/Immigration_and_Nationality_Act_of_1965

[22] https://en.wikipedia.org/wiki/Willmoore_Kendall

Stanley Parry, CSC, Eric Voegelin,[23] Gerhart Niemeyer,[24] Ralph McInerny,[25] and the itinerant German Aristotelian scholar, Henri Deku.[26]

After Richard Nixon's defeat in the 1960 presidential election, Harry Turner, a fellow member of Pitt's Young Republicans, brought a dozen back issues of *National Review* to a *YR* meeting and announced that though we had just lost a Presidential election, there was yet another battle to be waged, a battle to save America from "Liberalism." Turner and invited Bill Buckley to speak at Pitt, and we took him to a late lunch where he ordered a bottle of French Pomerol,[27] famous for its quality in Roman times --and picked up the luncheon tab.

That lunch began my association with Bill Buckley, members of his family (sisters Priscella Buckley and Carole Learsy) and writers for *National Review* (Frank Meyer, Mario Pei and others), who enlivened the "*Conservative Movement*" in the United States in the 1960s and 70s.

It was because of associations like these that I'm glad I did not pursue my studies at "*HYP*"—Harvard, Princeton or Yale.

"*HYP, of course,*" would have been better in Protestant America than this Roman Catholic University in a backwater city in Indiana.

---

[23] https://en.wikipedia.org/wiki/Eric_Voegelin

[24] https://isi.org/look-for-the-lift-a-biographical-essay-of-gerhart-niemeyer/

[25] https://en.wikipedia.org/wiki/Ralph_McInerny

[26] https://de.wikipedia.org/wiki/Henry_Deku

[27] https://en.wikipedia.org/wiki/Pomerol_AOC

My favorite example of South Bend, Indiana's culture is a liquor store that I frequented that discounted the price of red wine because the bottles were "dirty." I also remember complaining about South Bend to Eric Voegelin when a local movie theater was showing a movie about a husband planning to kill his wife. Voegelin observed that I should see the movie and "bone up."

Except for two graduates of Assumption College who also chose graduate studies at Notre Dame, and three Goldwater conservatives like Angelo Codevilla, Howard Segermark, and me, Notre Dame was not the place to go if you desired a teaching career at colleges that attracted exceptional students. The best Ph.D. from my graduate class, for instance, took a teaching job at Slippery Rock State in Pennsylvania.

I didn't give a damn about that!

The men under whom I studied at Notre Dame were the best that American higher education could offer a student who self-identified as a political conservative.

Even if Notre Dame was a "dead end" if you wanted to teach at a prestigious university, I had political aspirations and I knew these men could prepare even someone whose goal was to seek elective office.

My grandparents were "working class" immigrants from Germany and Armenia. Indeed, my father spoke Turkish until he learned to speak English in public school in Troy, NY, and grew up speaking English as a second language.

My mother's family were German Lutherans who emigrated to the United States and settled in Pittsburgh, Pennsylvania, where the dominant ethnic group was (and still is) German.

I was the first of their offspring to attend college, and my ambition to seek high elective office as a Republican from Pennsylvania was not something you would expect from someone from my family background. Why anyone in 1960, or even today, with a foreign name like Bishirjian thinks he might aspire to high elective office in the United States is a testament to the character of American politics and the fundamental fairness of the American people.

Until 1991 when the Soviet Union collapsed, variants of Socialism or the political religion of Marxism-Leninism dominated American higher education. That may explain why, if I am adversarial in disposition, I had to live in a culture where Marxism and Liberalism impeded my answering the important questions I had about politics and order.

Pittsburgh Pennsylvania also had reached its apogee and other centers of commerce and industry began to be called "home." In 1960, however, none could predict changes in technology that were to come, nor their impact, but by the year 1965, my hometown of Pittsburgh was a city whose best years were in a distant past. Past leaders of industry and commerce—Mellon,[28] Carnegie,[29] and Rockefeller,[30] and Frick[31]—had been dead for close to a century. Banking, steel production, and commerce flourished elsewhere. By the year 2000, Pittsburgh's "fat lady" had sung her last song and US Steel Corporation was ripe for takeover.

---

[28] https://en.wikipedia.org/wiki/Andrew_Mellon

[29] https://en.wikipedia.org/wiki/Andrew_Carnegie

[30] https://en.wikipedia.org/wiki/John_D._Rockefeller

[31] https://en.wikipedia.org/wiki/Henry_Clay_Frick

I didn't know that in 1960 when I was admitted as an undergraduate at the University of Pittsburgh, but the election of a Liberal Catholic politician from Massachusetts as President of the United States in the 1960 Presidential election set the tone of American life for two decades to come.

The society of English Protestants that founded America and had given us a written Constitution had been challenged, and bets on what the future would bring were "off." Business, Department Stores, Elementary and Secondary schools, Railroads, Christian churches and the faith they fostered took new directions—all began to transition to a new order which, for me, was less than compelling.

Though the places where American capital goods were produced had changed, the "Progressive"[32] ideology of Liberalism endured from its origin in the Progressive movement in the first decade of the 20th century and I, therefore, was out of step with "the smart money" that dominated American society and culture. But I had bet on the right horse, so to speak, and never regretted the promise—even with all its limitations—of an earned Ph.D. degree from Notre Dame.

The primary limitation of a Notre Dame Ph.D. is that Notre Dame is "Catholic."

Americans are subliminally anti-Catholic.

Catholic research universities cannot compete for talented scholars who prefer positions at secular universities. Consequently, my Notre Dame Ph.D. led me to accept teaching positions at prestige-less colleges—a new, nominally Catholic university, in Irving,

---

[32] https://en.wikipedia.org/wiki/Progressive_Era

Texas (University of Dallas), and a Catholic woman's college in New Rochelle, NY.

At my first teaching position in 1968 in the Department of Politics at the University of Dallas, none could replace Willmoore Kendall.[33] Kendall had died the year before in 1967, and after his death, I was the first full-time hire at $14,000 a year. Except for University of Dallas professors Melvin Bradford and Thomas Landess—two of my colleagues in UD's Politics and Literature Ph.D. degree program—there was no place for an aspiring political theorist like me, especially when Willmoore Kendall's replacement in UD's Department of Politics was Paul Eidelberg, [34] a "Straussian."

The division between Straussian and Voegelinian scholars is very great, so it was only a matter of time before the differences between Kendall's Straussian successor and me would lead to Non-Renewal of my contract after three years of service to the department. Moreover, UD's Politics program was soon dominated by "Straussians," and the one other Ph.D. in Politics from Notre Dame made fun of my argument in my Ph.D. dissertation, following Voegelin, that modernity is "gnostic".[35] After UD, I was fortunate to find another teaching position where for eight years I was able to practice what I was trained to do—at a Catholic woman's college in New Rochelle, New York.

In 1980, I accepted an appointment in the Reagan Administration and never returned to college teaching until I founded Yorktown University in 2000—twenty years later.

---

[33] https://en.wikipedia.org/wiki/Willmoore_Kendall

[34] https://en.wikipedia.org/wiki/Paul_Eidelberg

[35] https://voegelinview.com/modern-political-religion/

Though Ronald Reagan was an improvement over Presidents like Jimmy Carter, not all was well in Reagan's government.

Ronald Reagan's lack of experience in Government—like Donald Trump in 2016—would lead to later problems. President Reagan also had personal qualities that led to problems within the White House and lack of coordination among federal agencies.

In 1980, Reagan's advisors created "Transition Teams" to assess all government agencies, and I was chosen to lead the Transition Team for the National Endowment of the Humanities. As an unknown scholar, I was an unlikely choice—there weren't many politically active conservative Republicans in Academe—then or now.

But my part-time employer in nearby New Rochelle, the conservative publisher Arlington House, covered my expenses. As a result, I was able to accept appointment to "The Transition," even though my combined salary at Arlington House and as an assistant professor of political science at the College of New Rochelle wasn't sufficient to spend even a few days, not to mention weeks, in Washington, D.C.

Unlike the Republican Party and most top appointees of the Reagan Administration, Reagan's "Transition Teams" were composed of political conservatives, some going back as far as the 1952 Taft campaign, and many had served on each of Reagan's three attempts to become President. As "Political Directors" of a successful Presidential campaign, they would, in normal times, have a veto over political appointments and a choice of top assignments, if they chose to serve.

It became clear quite early, however, that Ronald Reagan's Administration would not follow the normal practice. The Chief of

Staff to his opponent, George H. W. Bush, was assigned to a team of three advisors to the President, and James Baker ultimately became Chief of Staff to the President. In other words, a "Moderate" Republican, not known for conservative views, became the chief gatekeeper of the Office of the President.

A key to Ronald Reagan's personality was the devastating experience of being a child of an alcoholic parent. That experience burned into him patterns of behavior common to children of alcoholics—dislike and avoidance of controversy, fear of confrontation and, for many children of alcoholics, an obsession with order. Reagan, thus, disliked confrontation, and when confronted with egregious violations of his political philosophy by his appointees, he did nothing.

Previous Presidents actively engaged in the selection of their top appointees right down to the assistant secretary level of government agencies. Dwight Eisenhower was known for taking a keen interest in mistakes made by his appointees and acted quickly to repair any damage that was done. When Nelson Rockefeller sent a short list of names to Richard Nixon asking that he consider them for appointment to his Administration, Nixon met with each and personally evaluated their qualifications.

A similar list was sent to Ronald Reagan, but the President-Elect did not interview them, nor did he play an active role in making appointments. I, myself, was advised to expect a call to meet with the President when nominated to an Assistant Secretary-level position.

That call never came.

The only time I met President-Elect Ronald Reagan was when James Baker and Ed Meese brought him to a gathering of members of his Transition Teams, where we were told not to expect appointments in Reagan's Administration.

As a political scientist, I knew very well from experience and study of the works of Plato that philosopher kings[36] are hard to find. But, I knew also about political patronage, and the persons who staffed the first few years of White House personnel in the Reagan Administration were oblivious to the need to salt the Administration with political conservatives. Margo Carlisle, a movement conservative and executive director of the Senate Steering Committee, told me, "They [Reagan's men] are not conservatives."

Of these men, James Baker was a moderate Republican. Michael Deaver had no permanent political views except loyalty to Ronald Reagan. Edwin Meese, an attorney, brought to the White House his experience as a former prosecutor in the district attorney's office of Alameda County, California, loyalty to Ronald Reagan but little else. Anyone looking at this lineup of White House talent would, therefore, conclude that conservative philosophy wasn't going to play an important role in the appointment process.

Nevertheless, as the year 1981 was ushered in, the Reagan Administration was the only game in town, and my 1960's generation of Goldwater conservatives began to attempt to identify where in Ronald Reagan's government we could best use our talents. About this time, I was asked to appear on a panel with Norman Podhoretz, editor of *Commentary*, at a meeting in New York of the Philadelphia Society. My presentation dealt with foreign policy and American

---

[36] https://en.wikipedia.org/wiki/Philosopher_king

values.[37] America's religious traditions, I argued, tended to lead us into attempts to replace balance of power politics with a "New World Order" of international law and democratic evangelism that could make the United States a principal cause of disorder in international politics.

Norman Podhoretz and I were introduced by Frank Shakespeare,[38] former director of USIA in the Nixon Administration, who gave a stirring introduction correctly identifying the importance of this convergence of so many conservatives at this one meeting of the Philadelphia Society. At earlier meetings of the Society, we were lucky if fifty to seventy-five people showed up. This meeting, though, was a sell-out crowd, with several hundred people filling the ballroom of New York's Essex House. Our panel was a good one, among the many held that day, but these folks were not there to hear Norman and me. They were there to get jobs in the Reagan Administration.

I was one of them.

After that panel presentation, Frank Shakespeare mentioned that I should seriously consider going after a job at USICA, the United States International Communication Agency (formed in 1978 when the US Information Agency (USIA) merged with the Bureau of Educational Cultural Affairs of the Department of State). The incumbent Associate Director for Education and Cultural Affairs at USICA under President Carter was Alice Ilchman[39] who later

---

[37] https://phillysoc.org/tps_meetings/u-s-foreign-policy-and-national-security/

[38] https://en.wikipedia.org/wiki/Frank_J._Shakespeare

[39] https://en.wikipedia.org/wiki/Alice_Stone_Ilchman

became president of Wellesley College. Shakespeare thought that with my education and political credentials, as well as my service on the NEH transition team, I ought to have a leg up on that position.

Because I had given up practical politics except for election as a local Republican Committeeman in Tarrytown, New York, I knew little about these things. Government service had not entered my mind since 1961 when I had a summer job as a GS-3 Clerk Typist at the General Services Administration.

But Frank Shakespeare's advice appealed to my ego, and I began a campaign to get the White House Office of Presidential Personnel to submit my nomination to the U.S. Senate for confirmation. Shakespeare assured me that this was an important job, so important, he said, that I could expect to be interviewed personally by President Reagan. In this, Shakespeare gave President Reagan too much credit: There was no interview by the President of me, nor of any sub-cabinet nominees in the entire Reagan Administration. President Reagan was simply ignorant of the nuts and bolts, day-to-day workings of his government.

I appreciated that Frank Shakespeare thought I should seek an appointment at USICA. But more hard-headed minds like Irving Kristol[40] thought it would be best if I were to go after a lower-level appointment that didn't require Senate confirmation. "You would be good," Kristol said, "and it's your due for an appointment as director of the education division of NEH." In a chance meeting with Ed Rollins,[41] I was advised to stay clear of Charles Z. Wick,[42] Nancy

[40] https://en.wikipedia.org/wiki/Irving_Kristol

[41] https://en.wikipedia.org/wiki/Ed_Rollins

[42] https://en.wikipedia.org/wiki/Charles_Z._Wick

Reagan's close friend, rumored to be seeking the appointment of Director of USICA.

Irving Kristol and Ed Rollins were right.

As I looked more deeply into the matter, however, other problems appeared. A friend who served as a special assistant to the President in the Office of Presidential Personnel told me that when she heard that I wanted that job, she didn't think I had a chance.

Frank Shakespeare, dismayed by Wick's interest in directing USICA, wanted the documentary producer and former assistant to Richard Nixon, Bruce Herschenson,[43] to be appointed its director. But Herschenson wasn't chosen. His problem and the problem of many other qualified conservatives seeking Presidential appointments turned upon the character of White House personnel. In a philosophically-driven administration, the head of an agency would have to share the President's political philosophy. The Reagan Administration's personnel shop, contrary to popular belief, was not philosophically driven.

As it turned out, Wick's desire to be head of USICA was more than just rumor. Bob Carter, a District of Columbia Republican Party official, who headed up the Transition Team for the National Endowment of Arts, had also served at the Inaugural Committee where Charles Z. Wick was co-chairman. Wick told Bob Carter that he was interested in having some information about NEH or NEA, was given the transition team reports, and decided that there wasn't enough "action" for him in either of those two positions. So, Bob Carter said, "Charlie, why don't you take a look at USICA."

---

[43] https://en.wikipedia.org/wiki/Bruce_Herschensohn

Wick was not a political conservative, far from it, but his wife was Nancy Reagan's closest friend. Wick graduated from the University of Michigan (B.M.) and Case Western Reserve University School of Law (J.D.). He was a member of the California and Ohio Bar Associations. He had been a pianist with one of the big bands when he was young and worked as an agent with a top talent agency in Hollywood. A less lawyer-like personality couldn't be found unless the word "attorney" conjures up such adjectives as "flamboyant," "ruthless," "ill-tempered," and "unstable." Admittedly, Wick did have an artistic bent as seen in his production of a film entitled *Snow White and the Three Stooges.*[44] Moreover, he was short—about 5'0"—and had a classic small man's personality—rude, abusive to those under him, and, I later surmised, unstable.

In most presidential administrations, a person with Charlie Wick's resume wouldn't stand a chance of any appointment. Wick, however, had done loyal service on behalf of "the Governor," raising money for his presidential campaigns. When Reagan was asked by his advisors—Meese, Baker, and Deaver—not to appoint Wick to head up USICA, Reagan is reported to have said, "After what Charlie did for me, he can have anything he wants." I can confirm that, as I once confronted James Baker, telling him to "fire Charlie Wick."

Baker responded, "*You* tell that to the President."

Charles Z. Wick wanted to become head of USICA and that meant trouble for political conservatives.

---

[44] https://en.wikipedia.org/wiki/Snow_White_and_the_Three_Stooges

For those of us conservative anti-Communists who studied American foreign policy during the Cold War, the "public diplomacy" of United States Information Agency (USICA's changed back to USIA in August 1982) was extremely important. That was where broadcasts of the Voice of America (VOA) were transmitted via shortwave behind the Iron Curtain to the captive nations of East and Central Europe. That agency oversaw all United States cultural centers and libraries throughout the world, and that agency presented daily press and information briefings to all U.S. embassies worldwide in a daily wire transmission called the "wireless file." That agency also conducted programs that represented the United States to the world—intellectually, culturally, and artistically. For those of us raised on Richard Weaver's maxim, "Ideas have consequences," this agency had an important role representing the idea of America to the world.

For that reason, we conservatives ranked USICA very high on the list of U.S. government agencies where we wanted to serve. As I found out after accepting the appointment to that position, Sen. William Fulbright thought so also. He summoned me to his office where he informed me that my position was the most important in the entire federal government![45]

A good foreign policy, if it is to be cohesive, must have similar minds at the National Security Council, Department of State, Defense, the Central Intelligence Agency, and USICA. The Administration of Ronald Reagan, however, had its NSC and State

---

[45] https://theimaginativeconservative.org/2018/03/how-got-fired-reagan-white-house-richard-bishirjian.html#_ftn1

Department working against the U.S. Department of Defense under Caspar Weinberger[46] and CIA Director William Casey.[47]

Constantine Menges' important book *Inside the National Security Council*[48] documents how U.S. Secretary of State George Shultz and National Security Council Advisor Robert McFarlane and White House Chief of Staff, James Baker, colluded with one another to steer a softer foreign policy toward the Soviet Union than that advocated by Casey, Weinberger, and Jeanne Kirkpatrick,[49] the U.S. ambassador to the United Nations.

All that came later since, at the time I sought an appointment in the Reagan Administration, Richard Allen,[50] for whom I had worked one summer at the Center for Strategic Studies, was Reagan's first NSC Advisor. He called Charles Z. Wick and told him to pick me. Nothing happened, though. Not relying solely on Dick Allen, I asked every conservative I knew to write to the White House on my behalf. But, still, nothing happened. I called Dick Allen again, and he agreed to pressure Wick, once again, to hire me. Only then did I receive a telephone call from Gilbert Robinson, Charlie Wick's Deputy, and I was invited to meet Gil Robinson—not Charlie Wick—in Washington.

Gilbert Robinson was a New York "Rockefeller" Republican who did not bring a conservative political philosophy nor administrative

---

[46] https://en.wikipedia.org/wiki/Caspar_Weinberger

[47] https://en.wikipedia.org/wiki/William_J._Casey

[48] https://www.amazon.com/stores/Constantine-Christopher-Menges/author/B001HPGQZU

[49] https://en.wikipedia.org/wiki/Jeane_Kirkpatrick

[50] https://en.wikipedia.org/wiki/Richard_V._Allen

experience to USICA. Both, I realized after my first few weeks at USICA, were needed. After a series of firings of conservative political appointees at USICA by Wick, including Philip Nicolaides, Kenneth Tomlinson, and me, Wick fired his Deputy, Gilbert Robinson. Robinson understandably resented being fired by Wick and turned confessor to New York Times columnist, William Safire, who exposed Wick's high crimes including illegal taping of telephone conversations, appointment of the children of Cabinet members, and the hiring of his own cronies, including his piano teacher and his tennis coach.

Wick was what is called "an accident waiting to happen," and the fact that he was so close to Ronald Reagan exacerbated the likelihood that bad publicity would tar the President. But, Wick wasn't the only problem. During preparations for the Inaugural, which Wick co-chaired, I learned from a former colleague at Arlington House Publishers, one who worked in the area where tickets that had been sold were kept in a walk-in safe, that Mary Jane Wick[51] went into the safe and removed tickets. I presume those tickets were needed by Nancy Reagan, but they were sold to political donors before she expressed her desires to distribute them to her friends. Hundreds of people arrived from all over the United States to attend Inaugural events only to be told that their tickets were nowhere to be found.

That was a problem that Washington's media elite could have used to destroy the President's popularity. Members of Congress thought so, too, and they decided an investigation of improprieties

---

[51] https://www.legacy.com/us/obituaries/latimes/name/mary-wick-obituary?id=22770422

of the Inaugural Committee were required before Charles Z. Wick's nomination to USICA could be taken up. As matters transpired, worse things occurred. On March 30, 1981, an assassination of President Reagan was attempted. I was teaching that day in class at the College of New Rochelle, a small Catholic woman's college in Westchester County, New York, and I recall one of my Liberal faculty colleagues saying sympathetically, that "They shot him before he even had a chance."

I think sorrow, upset, and a keen sense of loss were the universally felt experiences on that day—except at the U.S. Department of State. A friend, who was serving at the State Department in a minor political appointment had the opportunity to observe what the career foreign service officers experienced. It wasn't sadness. Some of State's "Officers" speculated about the physics and velocity of the bullets that struck the President, offering muted expression of interest about how seriously he was injured and speculating about his successor's policies.

As an observer of American national politics, I am aware that the best and the brightest don't go into government service. You find four basic types of people employed by the federal government:

1. Persons who want job-security;
2. Persons who are "do-gooders";
3. Persons whose sexual orientation require civil service protection; and
4. A smaller, but potentially more powerful, group who are enthusiasts of big, redistributionist, government.

At the U.S. Department of State, Agency for International Development, Environmental Protection Agency, Consumer Protection Agency, U.S. Department of Education, and many other agencies of the federal government, the last of these types prevail in positions where they can influence public policy, unless closely supervised by political appointees.

Most are extremely intelligent and better educated than other federal government workers and come to government service with advanced degrees from prestige universities that, with the Progressive movement, have encouraged idealistic youth to pursue academic disciplines for which the only employers are local, state, and federal governments. The influx of these key people in the federal government by the time Ronald Reagan was elected was certainly spurred by the personnel policies of the Kennedy Administration's idealism—"Ask not what your country can do for you, ask what you can do for your country," and the Johnson Administration's War on Poverty. People for whom those appeals resonated were not happy with the election of Ronald Wilson Reagan.

At USICA, my tenure was made difficult by foreign service "Officers" who placed a burden of proof on us. One senior executive, wife of Sen. Fulbright's chief of staff, asked me to a meeting where she proposed I endorse the decisions of her Directorate. I informed her that Ronald Reagan won the election, and since I am his surrogate, I will make all decisions. So, we political appointees of the President of the United States had to "prove" our good intentions to those for whom a regular government salary was vested. This was especially the case in the Educational Affairs directorate where the remnants of Wilsonian idealism were alive and well and for whom the "Reagan people" were, literally, seen as the barbarians at the gate.

On reflection, that judgment wasn't entirely wrong when applied to Charles Z. Wick. Wick was a colossal, ignorant, abusive boor, and many of the people he personally chose to work for him were simply unqualified. His choice for Voice of America director had no sense whatsoever of the purpose of VOA. In a meeting with National Security Advisor Dick Allen, the new VOA head displayed such total ignorance that Allen simply walked away shaking his head.

By June 1981, my own political appointment was still not finalized when I arrived in Washington for my first meeting at USICA. Wick was in California, and I was introduced to John "Jock" Shirley, a career foreign service "officer" who served as Acting Director of USICA until Wick could be confirmed. Though Jock Shirley was a superior public executive, he represented the interests of the Foreign Service, not those of the President of the United States. A political appointee might have been brought in as "Acting" to hold things in place until Wick was confirmed, but that type of political thinking was never a high priority under Wick. Nevertheless, that was the condition of the agency at the time I was interviewed by a career State Department Officer!

Political appointees have a special purpose in the order of Presidential administrations. They represent the President of the United States who was elected by the people in a Presidential election. Their purpose is to administer government agencies and design new policies in keeping with the philosophy of government of the newly elected President.

At USICA, under Wick, there was a conscious blurring of identity between political and career executives. This put me, the one political conservative appointee at USICA, at a disadvantage because Wick didn't understand this basic principle. He truly thought that the vast apparatus that he was to manage would simply, well, function on autopilot. He did not appreciate the need to put the President's men—men who were philosophically compatible with the principles of the newly-elected President—in all key positions by means of the political appointment process.

In my presence, Wick referred to himself as a "moderate," which was an honest statement, if shocking to those of us who had worked for the conservative Barry Goldwater and the conservative Ronald Reagan. Wick's former piano teacher whom he had hired to work at USICA told me that Wick had contributed $50,000 to the Campaign for President of George McGovern in 1972. That was a seismic election that drove important "Neoconservatives" into the Republican Party. But, Wick had supported a politician far to their Left!

After my first meeting at USICA, I returned to New York and waited for the call to join the Reagan Administration. Nothing happened for two months, but in April 1981—five months after the Presidential election—I was invited to meet with Wick himself.

My wife-- whom I later divorced--and I made the trip to Washington where we went to lunch with Charles Z Wick. All was pleasant, but I suspected that Wick resented that I was there because the President's National Security Advisor, Richard Allen, had pressured Wick to do something. I shall never forget that when lunch ended, Wick rose from his chair and assisted my wife into her jacket. Before he placed the coat in reach, he flipped the jacket's label to check who the designer was!

The application process for political appointees is intrusive, and Wick could have asked for my financial forms that I had to submit. As a college teacher, I had no assets to speak of, no stocks nor bonds, just a salary and a vested retirement account with TIAA-CREF, the retirement fund established by Andrew Carnegie for teachers. My wife's background could have killed my aspiration to serve President Reagan, but did not.

I must have passed the "designer test," however, because in May 1981, I was told that I could start work on June 1—but I would be placed in a back room until I passed a full FBI field investigation. I didn't think this would be a problem since I had studiously avoided doing something stupid like visiting the Soviet Union as a tourist. And, as a conservative with credentials going back to 1961, I was hardly likely to be a communist agent.

I returned to New York once again and when word came to move to D.C., I packed my car for the trip and planned to stay with friends for several weeks. That was seven months *after* Ronald Reagan's election. Delays in processing all the forms necessary for political appointees to take office is a real problem for new Presidential Administrations. A new president is elected, but it is not possible to clear people for work at the Assistant Secretary level until five, seven, or even twelve months after the election! It is not difficult to understand why the delay. "Watergate," and the special legislation that was generated by that scandal, slowed down the process by which a President may fill appointive positions.

All this is silly, of course.

We will have crooks and thieves with us always.

What is central, however, is that they be loyal to a President elected by the people of the United States. Moreover, we must ask ourselves, "Are we running a church or a country?" How high a standard do we want to set for public service? How high can we set that standard without major ill-effects on government itself? Should the standards for political appointments be set so high that no normal, sane person will seek appointive office?

The conservative attitude, founded on the theological principle of Original Sin, is that man is flawed, weak, and prone to sin. Man is easily tempted and knowingly yields to temptation. Man will break God's laws, violate basic standards of morality, and Man will violate the laws of the United States. During the selection process for Presidential appointees, we have seen that any violation of law can terminate the confirmation of nominees who retain babysitters, and personal servants, without making payroll withholding deposits. Failure to report income for purposes of taxation, inside trading, conflicts of interest, membership in private clubs that discriminate against minorities, DUI convictions—all are standards that can cause a nomination to withdraw from consideration.

Frankly, based on my experience in government, all the above are acceptable failures that are outweighed by *loyalty* to the President of the United States. The object upon the election of a President should be to fill all political offices in good time, say, two months—not two years. If that means that some full field investigations have to be double, triple, or quadruple staffed at great cost, then so be it.

And if, after a full field investigation, somebody passes an FBI and OPM investigation that misses a serious misdeed, then we should take that as the price for having to deal with human beings. If they are above room temperature, they will have made mistakes, and we should worry about their personal problems later. If, on the other hand, they haven't made mistakes, then we should not put them in public service because they are motivated by ideological or personal commitments that transcend the public interest of the United States.

For what purpose do the American people hold elections for a President anyway? If it takes two years of painstaking research, reports, investigation, and press scrutiny before a new President can have his people in place, why not simply dispense with elections and allow the career bureaucrats to run the government?

Mid-day on May 31, 1981, I loaded my car with books, a lamp, and a suitcase and drove one last time to the College of New Rochelle to pay my respect to two close faculty friends. One of them asked when I would come back and I replied, "I hope, never." So, off I drove south on I-95 toward Washington, D.C., to take a presidential appointment at the United States International Communication Agency. What I was to do or what waited for me, I had no idea.

I arrived at the USICA office—then at 1776 Pennsylvania Avenue, NW—a block from the White House, was sworn in, had my fingerprints taken, and given an empty office. Wick was still in California, awaiting word to come to Washington for his confirmation hearings. In the meantime, there wasn't much for me to do in that empty office. I had no authority, but I did my best to use my skills as a teacher, researcher, and writer to acquire as much information as I could. This involved reading the briefing materials that had been compiled for political appointees. I then began to interview members of the Education bureau's professional staff.

I also attended 8:00 am meetings with Wick's Deputy Director and tried as best I could to put together a staff of dedicated political appointees. This wasn't as easy as I had thought it would be since the other political appointees made no attempt to hire political appointees. They relied on the career staff, so my requests to hire "politicals" raised eyebrows and "concerns." I moved quickly, however, and was able to retain a special assistant; staff assistant; director of educational programs; director of private sector programs; and director of libraries and culture centers.

In a very short time, I had a working, functioning, politically sound operation ready and able to take on all and any tasks required of the Associate Director for Educational and Cultural Affairs. By contrast, none of the other Associate Directors saw the need to staff their offices with reliable conservative political appointees. As a result, when it dawned on Director Wick that he needed to do something in confidence that wouldn't be leaked to the Washington Post, he turned to my staff for support. As well he should. Charlie Wick was in deep Doo-Doo.

His nomination was being held up, and he arrived in Washington in late June without knowing when he might be confirmed by the U.S. Senate. I assumed that he was confident that he would be confirmed since Ronald Reagan wanted him in Wick's choice of where Wick felt he could contribute to the Administration. But the bad odor Wick had created by the manner he treated subordinates caused me to doubt if he would make it through a rigorous confirmation process. I met with Wick regularly during those hot summer days in personal meetings and by telephone when he was in California.

In August 1981, prior to a presentation to the National Security Council that Wick had requested, Wick asked me and my staff to put together a proposal titled "Operation Truth." I immediately called friends and former colleagues including Angelo Codevilla, then a professional staff member of the Senate Intelligence Committee, an assistant to Dick Allen at the NSC, the Undersecretary of Defense, Fred Ikle, and a principal assistant to Ed Meese. We agreed to meet, whereupon I asked them to design a counter disinformation campaign. They responded within days, and I submitted the proposal to Wick for his approval. "Operation Truth" was born.

The President and the NSC loved it, and the president signed a presidential directive making it one of the first policies of the Reagan Administration.

In the normal course of government service, I would take comfort knowing that I had done my job. But it became obvious that Wick was a "taker," not a "giver."

While away in California, Wick came up with the idea that there should be an initiative to the private sector. Guided by JFK's phrase, "Ask not what your country can do for you, ask what you can do for your country," Wick decided to ask top-level private sector leaders to volunteer services and material. Wick meant by this "volunteerism" that he would "take" from the private sector what was needed to reduce his agency's operating costs!

In other words, Wick intended to set up private sector committees to which the "best and brightest" in America would be asked to make a contribution.

USICA had libraries, so let's have the best and brightest publishers tell us how to improve our library holdings.

USICA had cultural centers, so let's have a private sector committee devoted to "Culture."

I was very cautious about this idea since most people who make a living in books and culture were not friendly toward Ronald Reagan. And Wick should have been concerned that these committees would be perceived as opportunities to get something from the government by those who volunteered their services.

Since USICA was in the "advertising business," as Wick often said, he called a meeting at which all the best and brightest advertising men from New York showed up as well as Jack Valenti, former LBJ special assistant, and Sonny Werblin, head of Madison Square Gardens.

None were vetted for their conservative views.

Wick's desire was to set up a broad range of committees to which prominent Americans contributed their knowledge and expertise. Since Wick could never articulate exactly what he meant, Wick's Deputy didn't understand what Wick was getting at either.

Wick turned on his Deputy shouting "What about my private sector committees?" I took the Deputy's side and said, "Don't worry Charlie, we'll take care of it."

Wick then tore into me in full view of all present. "What do you mean? Why hasn't this been done?"

I was embarrassed, of course, but I was also troubled since Wick had violated a basic rule of civility. If you have a problem with someone, you discuss it in private—not in public. During a fire drill, Wick dressed down a clerk he saw outside the building holding a "Secret" folder. Technically, that was a violation of security regulations, but the manner in which Wick acted called into question his emotional stability.

On another occasion, the Associate Director for Administration took the brunt of Wick's wrath. As we met early in the morning, Wick wanted to know what had been done about his suggestion of a few weeks previous. He found it hard to find the right words for what he wanted done, but ultimately it became clear that Wick wanted "Suggestion Boxes" placed near each of the elevators in the Agency building.

To his credit, the Director for Administration said, "Mr. Wick, I joined the Reagan Administration to make a difference in policy, not to install suggestion boxes." Wick immediately turned on him, shouting "If you want a job by noon today, those Suggestion Boxes better be installed."

Wick was, quite simply, unstable, yet both he and Mary Jane Wick had ingratiated themselves with the President and would holiday with the Reagans at Thanksgiving and Christmas.

Nevertheless, with my staff being the only politically reliable office in the building, I was called upon by Wick to provide the type of confidential work that he couldn't allow his own Front Office staff to do because he was literally surrounded by career foreign service "officers." Even his General Counsel was a career civil servant.

The head of Voice of America told me, as he snapped his fingers to a rhythm only he could hear, that he was seeking a "sound for the 80s," yet he was clearly over his head, so he was asked to work with a political appointee who was politically conservative and had communication experience. Philip Nicolaides[52] was asked to help keep the VOA director from doing anything more to rile the conservatives who, by now, had sized up Wick's management of USICA and were calling for changes. Nicolaides had worked on Jim Buckley's successful campaign for the United States Senate and had a very long record of campaign work going back to 1964. Joseph Sobran had described Nicolaides as "a splendid singer, a gifted artist, a pianist, a linguist, a wit, all in all the most charming, entertaining, talented man most of his friends (including me) had ever met."

I was told by a friend from New York who had worked on the staff of National Review that Nicolaides was a good guy and that I could talk to him in confidence. Nicolaides and I ultimately broke out some private time to be together and sized one another up. Nicolaides ventured to suggest that, maybe, something was terribly wrong at USICA. Trusting the recommendation of my friend, I told him, "Wick is the problem." Nicolaides and I became fast friends, so seldom is honesty practiced within the federal government.

Unfortunately, Nicolaides had been out of government too long and forgot that anything with his name on it could be used against him. He made the mistake of composing a memorandum to the director of VOA—which he had been asked to do—on a computer that could be accessed by anyone in his office. Someone accessed the Nicolaides file that said, basically, that VOA has a political function to perform.

---

[52] http://www.fgfbooks.com/Sobran-Joe/2019/Sobran190628.html

The Washington Post obtained a copy of the memorandum and splashed a headline across the front page of the Washington Post—"VOA Official Politicizes Agency."

In Washington, D.C., the word "politicize" is similar to the word "defile," and upon hearing that word, grown Liberals weep, fearing the rise of Nazi and Fascist forces in America. Fortunately, the miscreant Nicolaides had been discovered, lurking within that bastion of truth, objectivity and press freedom, the U.S. government's Voice of America.

Politicizing the entire American government had been conducted robustly from FDR, through Harry Truman, through JFK, perfected by LBJ and refined to an art form by Richard Nixon. Upon becoming President, Nixon's successor, Gerald Ford, established a "Charter" at the Voice of America requiring that all reports emanating from that source be "objective." From that day forward, all VOA broadcasts would tell America's story—"warts and all." As a result, VOA reporters had nothing to fear by telling how bad America had become under Ronald Reagan. And they loved doing that.

Nicolaides, sensing the danger in this anti-American bias of the Foreign Service, recommended that VOA should tell the good side of America before slamming her in VOA daily broadcasts. For that, Phil Nicolaides was forced to resign. That occurred during the second month of Wick's tenure.

Nicolaides knew that the commitment of political Liberals to extend democracy to all parts of the world was not in the national interest of the United States and that telling a story that America intends to do just that is "ideological" and not representative of the American political tradition—at least until Woodrow Wilson put his hand to reshaping that tradition. Nicolaides tried to modify VOA thinking to conform to a traditional conservative view and paid for that with loss of his service in the Reagan Administration.

All was not well elsewhere in the Agency, particularly in the Bureau of Programs. The head of the Directorate for Programs was a former Editor for the Christian Science Monitor and a Pulitzer Prize winner. As far as I could see, the new Director of Programs was a decent enough chap—for a Liberal journalist—but he was the wrong person to head up the Programs Bureau at USICA. Significantly, when he left USIA, he became George Shultz's press spokesman at the Department of State.

The Programs Division at USIA is labor intensive—lots of employees and a small budget. One of the functions of this division is to choose Americans to represent the United States abroad in functions requested, supervised, and scheduled by our public affairs officers in American Embassies throughout the world.

The American Participants division of the Programs Bureau, called "AmParts," was headed by a foreign service officer.

That was mistake number one. But, if you have a nitwit or political naïf at the head of the Agency and at the head of the Bureau your political appointee, you can expect problems to develop.

At first, I thought the suggestions from the Embassies as funneled to the Director's office through the Programs Bureau were a joke. There were requests for all types of fauna and flora on the Left-wing of American political life, and nothing that reflected the interesting changes on the American political landscape as expressed in the presidential election of 1980. Even Wick's Deputy thought this was a problem, and, in a meeting of the Bureau Directors, he suggested that the names of potential "AmParts" be circulated for review among the Bureau Directors.

The first few lists that I saw were testaments to serious problems in the bowels of the bureaucracy that the Programs Director should have taken care of himself by putting in a political appointee to screen recommendations before being sent up to the Director. Instead, these lists of names of prominent Americans to be invited to go abroad by USIA became formalized in a process that led ultimately to the forming of what apparently was a list of names of persons "proscribed" from representing the U.S. government during the presidency of Ronald Reagan. In other words, a process had been put into motion that led to the formation of an "enemies" list—or, at least, that was how the media and the Senate Foreign Relations Committee came to see the matter. No one among us in that small room wanted anything like that to occur, but the Deputy Director had to compensate for the failure of the Programs Director to act politically. Consequently, the entire executive suite of political appointees at USIA became tainted.

Ultimately, the Acting Deputy Director of USIA, neoconservative Leslie Lenkowsky, paid the supreme price for the Programs Director's failure when he was denied confirmation for politicizing USIA and maintaining a "hit" list or list of enemies. Obviously, Lenkowsky had done no such thing. His predecessor's naiveté allowed a career bureaucrat to maintain a list of names of people that political appointees suggested ought not to be programmed for USIA tours. When the president of the United States has initiated an economic policy that the press has dubbed "Reaganomics," and the whole world wanted to know what that meant, then USIA should send Paul

Craig Roberts, Milton Friedman, Art Laffer and Jack Kemp abroad on tours aimed at letting people know what's up. The public affairs officers of USIA, without exception, therefore, called for leading Keynesians to be invited for such tours. Lenkowsky was unlucky enough to be denied confirmation because of the ineptitude of the career Foreign Service.

Wick could do, and did, anything he wanted in a madcap, almost deranged manner, simply because Ronald Reagan refused to allow anyone to persuade him that Wick had to go. Wick should never have been appointed and confirmed because of malfeasance at the Inaugural Committee. But, instead, every conservative of note was ultimately purged from USIA, and Wick stayed in office until Ronald Reagan flew off to California eight years after taking office in 1981. I last saw Charlie Wick in the procession at Ronald Reagan's funeral. Had I known this, I might have been inclined not to help Wick, but, rather, seek to undo him.

After awhile, observant conservatives in the Reagan Administration got the message and began to sabotage Liberals nominated by the White House. That was what my conservative friends successfully did at the Department of Education under U.S. Secretary of Education, Terrell Bell.

Bell, too, was a ridiculous appointment for a conservative President to make but appointed he was.

For my part, I did not leak Wick's mistakes to the press. I had been a loyal Republican for many years in my home state of Pennsylvania and later in New York where I was an elected Committeeman, and I never sought to unseat obnoxious Republicans during those years. 1 would never have been able get my work done, had I tried to do so, because there were so many. Life is not perfect, and neither are political parties. You work with what you've got, play with the hand you've been given, and do your loyal best.

When Wick expressed consternation to me in June, 1981 that yet another hold had been put on his nomination, I offered to do what I could and called Bill Timmons, a prominent Washington lobbyist, told him of the problem and asked for his advice. He told me that his partner, Tom Korologos, had gone to Senator Robert Byrd, (D-WVA) and asked that a hold be placed on Wick's nomination. Why? Because Wick had promised Korologos an appointment, with Senate confirmation, to the Board of Advisors of USIA, yet Korologos had not yet been appointed. The appointment was important to Korologos because he wanted to prove to the world—and to himself—that he could be confirmed by the U.S. Senate and because the appointment would enable him to travel all over the world on official US government business on a diplomatic passport. Not bad for a Washington lobbyist!

So, I went to Wick and told him why this latest setback occurred and how it could be resolved—simply honor his promise to Korologos.

By then, my loyal service to Wick should have endeared me to him, and my tenure at USICA would be assured as long as I wanted. Unfortunately, that was not to be. One day, I received a communication classified "Top Secret" issued by another government agency informing me about an issue that required a decision by Wick. At a meeting of my full staff, I outlined what Wick should decide. When presented to him, Wick was indifferent and members of the Foreign Service appeared not to care. Top Foreign Service Officers aspire to become Ambassadors, and the best way to achieve that goal is never to offend the foreign countries in which they serve.

With no support from Wick, nor his Foreign Service "Officers," I asked T. Kenneth Cribb, an assistant to Edwin Meese to take up the case with Meese. It was clear to me that if the wrong decision was made, a major scandal would embroil the President.

Meese's assistant clearly sensed the danger of my request, and asked, "Do you want me to give this to Meese?" I said, "Yes."

On Columbus Day, 1981, Wick asked me to meet him. I came to his office, and he said, "Did you go to the White House about this?" I admitted that I had done that. Wick immediately told me that I was fired. He had been in a meeting with Ed Meese and at the end of the meeting, Meese asked "What are you going to do about this?" Wick realized at that moment that he had a "problem" and within an hour had resolved it, not by taking the action I recommended, but by firing the person who alerted the White House to a problem that was in development because Wick had not acted.

The Foreign Service was delighted since I was clearly not on their side but loyally represented the conservative President. Wick couldn't have cared less since he was not a person who was cognizant of the dangers his inaction had fostered. And the staff that I had recruited were compelled to serve the balance of their tenure at USICA under politically astute Bureau heads who did nothing to advance the President's policies.

In 1980, having left CNR to serve Ronald Reagan, my chances of employment as a university instructor were not good. I effectively was "out" of University Education, but I remained dedicated to my calling as a political philosopher by publishing seven scholarly books and a novel about American politics. I also published more than fourteen essays in *Modern Age*[53] and essays in other intellectual journals including *The Imaginative Conservative,*[54] *Chronicles of Culture,*[55] *Voegelin View,*[56] *Humanitas,*[57] *The American Spectator,*[58] *The American Political Science Review,*[59] *The Journal of Politics,*[60] and the now defunct *Anamnesis.*[61]

Add to these publications three important lectures I gave at meetings of the Philadelphia Society:

U.S. Foreign Policy and American Values (1980)[62]
Culture and Politics (1982)[63]
The Pursuit of Wisdom in the Age of the Internet (2009)[64]

---

[53] https://modernagejournal.com/

[54] https://theimaginativeconservative.org/2019/01/coming-decline-fox-news-richard-bishirjian.html

[55] https://chroniclesmagazine.org/american-proscenium/scott-walkers-main-chance/

[56] https://voegelinview.com/conservatism-and-spiritual-and-social-recovery/

[57] https://www.pdcnet.org/humanitas

[58] https://spectator.org/

[59] https://www.cambridge.org/core/journals/american-political-science-review

[60] https://www.jstor.org/stable/2128963

[61] https://theimaginativeconservative.org/2012/08/a-review-of-review-anamnesis-journal.html

[62] https://phillysoc.org/tps_meetings/changes-in-the-intellectual-environment-since-world-war-ii/

[63] https://phillysoc.org/tps_meetings/changes-in-the-intellectual-environment-since-world-war-ii/

[64] https://phillysoc.org/voices-of-conservatism/?speaker_id=4987

As the Internet developed, I produced "Zoom" podcasts on such topics as "loss of country,"[65] "The Administrative State,"[66] and political conservatives who write novels.[67]

This comment on *Ennobling Encounters*[68] by Roger Stone captures my motivation throughout my professional life:

> "*Dick Bishirjian is one of the few individuals alive who can accurately chronicle the important rise and development of the modern conservative movement. Rising from the ashes of Barry Goldwater's 1964 defeat, the American conservative movement galvanized a new majority of voters who elected President Ronald Reagan to two terms, as well as winning the improbable victory of President Donald J. Trump. Bishirjian's candid and thoughtful analysis of giants like F. Clifton White, Arthur Finkelstein and Bill Buckley alone are well worth giving this important book a read. I highly recommend it to serious students of political history.*"[69]

So, how can I resume "My Story" without sounding vainglorious?

---

[65] https://www.youtube.com/watch?v=980uZWZskAg

[66] https://www.youtube.com/watch?v=r52ngCdVL2o

[67] https://www.youtube.com/watch?v=h0rwI0Cnmfo

[68] https://enroutebooksandmedia.com/ennoblingencounters/

[69] https://www.amazon.com/gp/customer-reviews/R3APM410PUST25/

Maybe by focusing on my service to the Conservative "movement" and highlighting that the first Presidential election in which I was engaged was the Nixon campaign for President of 1960.

At a meeting of Young Republicans at the University of Pittsburgh at which Ed Flaherty, chairman of the Allegheny County Republican Party, was speaker, I wrangled employment as an office boy. After classes at Pitt, I would go to Republican HQs and work the office switchboard. This was an exciting experience for an 18-year-old college kid, and I enjoyed every minute of that job and the men I met, including Ed Flaherty, Warren Tesauro, and Cong. Bob Corbett,[70] who arranged employment for me in Summer 1961 in the Office of George Gryc[71] at the General Services Administration (GSA) where I was a GS-3 Clerk Typist.

I came away from that experience with an understanding, reinforced later in my career, that government service was not for me. Yet tens of thousands of young Americans seek government jobs to "do good" for their fellow Americans—and for peoples of other countries. Their "doing good" has led too often to military action aimed at spreading "Democracy." I soon came to see that American National Government had become an "Administrative State" that was transforming American constitutional government from one that *governed* into a "Big Government" that *ruled* its subjects.

But I get ahead of myself.

Let's start with my history of political theory published in 1978 and which my University of Dallas colleague, Melvin Bradford,

---

[70] https://en.wikipedia.org/wiki/Robert_J._Corbett

[71] https://www.alaskareport.com/news58/x61215_george_gryc.htm

encouraged me to write. Professor Bradford's wife, Marie, prepared this history for publication.

The Development of Political Theory, published in 1978, is divided into four parts: Part One is a discussion of "Classical Christian Political Theory," followed by "Modern Political Theory," "Second Realities," and "Beyond Behaviorism." The section on "Second Realities" reflects my studies with Eric Voegelin who was in residence at Notre Dame during several semesters of my stay in graduate school there.

In an essay published in *VoegelinView,*[72] Palm Beach Atlantic University Prof. Linda Raeder traces the origins of Voegelin's concept of "Second Realities" to what she calls "the existential resisters" who "are dissatisfied with the lack of order they experience in personal and social existence." They manifest their dissatisfaction with reality, visible according to Dr. Raeder, in six ways that constitute a modern form of "gnosticism."

1. Dissatisfaction with present existence.
2. The belief that this dissatisfaction results from the intrinsically poor organization of the world. If something is not right, the reason is to be found in the evil of the world.
3. The belief that salvation from the wickedness of the world is possible.
4. The belief that the order of being will be changed in an historical solution, that a good world will evolve historically.

---

[72] https://voegelinview.com/voegelin-on-gnosticism-modernity-and-the-balance-of-consciousness/

5. The belief that a change in the order of being can be realized through human action, that "self-salvation" is possible through man's own effort.
6. The construction of a "formula" for self- and world-salvation based upon knowledge of how to alter being.

Part One of *The Development of Political Theory* necessarily addresses what came first in the historical development of classical Greek political theory—Anaximander, Socrates, Plato, and Aristotle.

That discussion is followed in Part Two with a discussion of modern political theorists Machiavelli, Hobbes, Locke and Rousseau. These first two parts of *The Development of Political Theory* are preceded by a discussion of cosmological myths, the break with "cosmological" symbolization of order by Anaximander and Socrates through Plato and Aristotle and my description of Christian political theory as "Philosophy of History."

All that is accomplished in 66 pages!

Of course that brevity was a young man's mistake, and I'd like to avoid a repetition here, but the best I can do is to introduce you to a fuller discussion in my 2018 essay, published in *VoegelinView*, entitled "Conservatism and Spiritual and Social Recovery."[73]

Had I wanted greater sales of copies of my history of political theory, I should never have mentioned Christianity. But I can't hide the fact that Western political philosophy is based in Christianity.

---

[73] https://voegelinview.com/conservatism-and-spiritual-and-social-recovery/

Rejection of Christianity is endemic to intellectual discourse in our day, so by stating that Western political order is Christian closes many, if not all doors, to interest in classical political theory. Indeed, even Thomas Molnar[74] published a review of *The Development of Political Theory*, criticizing my concept of "Classical Christian." Philosophy, Molnar wrote, is essentially nonreligious.

Fortunately, a Catholic publisher, En Route Books and Media,[75] is engaged in affirmation of Christianity and will publish a new edition.

After completing my Ph.D. dissertation in 1970, I was attracted to teaching at the University of Dallas because Willmore Kendall was chairman of the Department of Politics. In 1970, Kendall had published *The Basic Symbols of the American Political Tradition*[76] with Catholic University political theorist George Carey. But Kendall died in 1974. Upon arrival at UD, I was perceived as Kendall's replacement.

That was ridiculous, of course. I lasted three years.

I had to make a living, however, and was able to find employment at a Catholic woman's college, The College of New Rochelle,[77] in New Rochelle, New York, founded by the Ursuline religious order.

---

[74] https://en.wikipedia.org/wiki/Thomas_Molnar

[75] https://www.enroutebooksandmedia.com

[76] https://www.amazon.com/Basic-Symbols-American-Political-Tradition/dp/0813208262/

[77] https://en.wikipedia.org/wiki/College_osoplhylof_New_Rochelle

Quite quickly it occurred to me that, just maybe, I didn't belong in college level teaching because at CNR I came into conflict with CNR's president, Sr. Dorthy Ann Kelly, OSU.

Sr. Dorothy Ann was a political and theological Liberal who bridled at the hegemony of male priests and had little appreciation for education in general and no interest in political "conservatism." By opposing her intent to water down CNR's curricular standards which she proposed in order to adjust to changes in Catholic higher education, I earned her enmity--and the respect of my faculty colleagues. When the Reagan Administration offered me a Presidential appointment in 1980, I leapt at the offer as a way of escape from CNR.

When asked by my CNR colleagues, "When will you return?" I replied "Never, I hope." Indeed, I never returned to college teaching until twenty years later when I founded Yorktown University. N

I last saw Sr. Dorthy Ann at the entrance to the West Wing of the Reagan White House in 1981 where I offered to assist her in her efforts on behalf of CNR.

Though I left college teaching in 1980, I "stayed the course" by continuing my dedication to the role of a classical political theorist by interpreting what holds men together in political communities. That was the subject of the "Introduction" in my first book, a history of political philosophy.

Unfortunately, classic Greek Philosophy is not as infectious as French Rationalism which is contributing to the death of true pursuit of truth.

Beginning in 2000, I attempted a reform of American "higher" education by founding Yorktown University.

This story is told in my 2017 book entitled *The Coming Death and Future Resurrection of American Higher Education* (St. Augustine Press, 2017).[78]

Though I could not speak Polish or Czech, I worked in Poland and the Czech Republic—before the collapse of the Berlin Wall. There, I learned the value of the Internet by utilizing MCI Mail to communicate with Polish and Czech business managers. The state-controlled mail systems in Poland and what is now the Czech Republic would deliver my requests via Telex to meet with someone on staff who spoke English. I learned from that experience that meetings and discussions equivalent to university classes could take place via the Internet.

University courses could be taught without classrooms!

Why build or sustain university campuses at great cost when it costs less than $2 million to found internet-based institutions?

My story of Yorktown University is "bittersweet."

As "higher" education moved intellectually and politically "Leftward," conservative faculty who would have attracted conservative graduate students declined in numbers. As a consequence, intelligent conservative college students found employment in "Think Tanks," not in higher education, and did not pursue advanced academic degrees. I earned a Ph.D., but once I was identified as a political conservative, I could not easily find, nor did I try to find, a suitable university teaching position. The factionalism in the Reagan

---

[78] https://www.amazon.com/Coming-Future-Resurrection-American-Education/dp/1587312743

Administration also made service there untenable. My appointment at USICA was brief—from June to October, 1980.

Count Nikolaus Lobkowicz,[79] President of the Catholic University of Eichstätt in Bavaria Germany, and I were attendees at meetings of the Foreign Policy Discussion Group in Washington, DC, which led "Lob" to ask me to find financing to support orthodox Catholic academics in Poland and the Czech Republic. What I learned in Poland and the Czech Republic (before the collapse of the Berlin Wall) was used to finance a start-up, solely internet-based, University.

Though I spent a year in London writing a Ph.D. dissertation on Thomas Carlyle, I had never traveled to USSR-dominated Poland nor Czechoslovakia. But Lobkowicz needed my help, and I spent time in Warsaw and Prague assessing how I could pitch requests for donations of support from Americans.

I soon found that I loved Poland and the Polish people, but that American donors are not inclined to donate to foreign projects. *The Coming Death and Future Resurrection of American Higher Education* would not have been written, however, but for the time I spent in Prague and Warsaw on behalf of Count Lobkowicz. Nor would I have gained entrée to the community of German business executives were it not for the Lobkowicz family name.

The General Partner of the Bosch Corporation whom I met in Stuttgart is one example. Not only did he make a donation, but he introduced me to Henry Kissinger who agreed to give two lectures—Free of Charge! In my 2017 book, I describe my first meeting with

---

[79] https://www.oasiscenter.eu/en/nikolaus-lobkowicz-1

Henry Kissinger in his New York office and the disconnect between the new Marriott Hotel in Prague and canned Cuban Pineapple from Castro's Cuba in store windows.

Today college tuition in the United States is a political *hot potato* with frequent complaints about the high cost of a college degree. Based on my experience, in *Coming Death* I outline thirteen ways to reform higher education and reduce the high cost of a college diploma. More than a decade later I can add one more way—bring a "restraint of trade action" against the Regional Accrediting Agencies.

I published five scholarly books after the *Coming Death,* but the one I enjoyed most is *Coda,* a novel,[80] which my publisher described as dealing with "American Politics, Personal Loss, and Recovery."

There is an actual gallery named "CODA"[81] in Palm Desert, California that I visited and first saw the ceramic lady in a ball gown that inspired me to write the eponymous novel.

I once thought that scholars were unlikely novelists until I invited a group of them[82] to talk about the novels they have written.

In 2022, I published ***Ennobling Encounters*** as testimony to the courage and hard work that has gone into recovery from "Liberal" ideology by the men I encountered during my professional life. The conservative *enfant terrible,*[83] Roger Stone, gave *Ennobling Encounters* very high praise.

So ends the first part of *My Story.*

---

[80] https://enroutebooksandmedia.com/coda/

[81] https://codagallery.com/

[82] https://www.youtube.com/watch?v=h0rwI0Cnmfo

[83] https://www.merriam-webster.com/dictionary/enfant terrible

Part Two

After completing writing my Ph.D. dissertation in 1970, I was attracted to seek employment as an Assistant Professor of Politics at the University of Dallas because Willmoore Kendall was chairman of the Department.

In 1970, Kendall had published *The Basic Symbols of the American Political Tradition*[1] with Catholic University political theorist George Carey. *Basic Symbols* refocuses American politics from the Declaration of Independence to its more substantial basis in Western political history starting with Cicero, St. Augustine, and St. Thomas.

But Kendall died in 1974.

I was hired after several unsuccessful attempts by University of Dallas President, Donald Cowan and his wife, Louise Cowan, to hire an established academic as Kendall's replacement.

Apparently, my colleague, Professor Melvin Bradford, had been impressed when he visited my new Faculty office in Braniff and saw an Old English[2] dictionary on my office bookshelf. As a distinguished Professor of Literature, Bradford appreciated my interest in Old English, but Bradford was also knowledgeable about Eric Voegelin[3] and disapproved of the Straussian[4] emphasis on close

---

[1] https://www.amazon.com/Basic-Symbols-American-Political-Tradition/dp/0813208262/

[2] https://en.wikipedia.org/wiki/Old_English

[3] https://en.wikipedia.org/wiki/Eric_Voegelin

[4] See https://academic.oup.com/edited-volume/34508/chapter-abstract/292802884?redirectedFrom=fulltext&login=false

reading of classic texts because that method tended to ignore the political, theoretical, and historical truths they embodied.

As a student of Eric Voegelin, I was not a *Straussian*, and Bradford had high hopes for me. But I lasted only three years. I was not a "fit" for a program committed to Agrarian literature. I realized that and joked about the several years I lived in the South—Miami, Florida.

I had to make a living but was able to find employment only at a Catholic woman's college, the College of New Rochelle,[5] in New Rochelle, New York, founded by the Ursuline religious order.

Quite quickly, it occurred to me that just maybe I didn't belong in college level teaching because at the College of New Rochelle I came into immediate conflict with CNR's president, Sr. Dorothy Ann Kelly, OSU.

Sr. Dorothy Ann was a political and theological Liberal who bridled at the hegemony of male Catholic priests, had little understanding of the importance of Catholic education, and saw in me everything she detested.

By opposing her intent to water down CNR's curricular standards in order to increase enrollments, I earned Sr. Dorothy Ann's enmity, but I also earned the respect of my faculty colleagues. When the Reagan Administration offered me a Presidential appointment in 1980, however, I leapt at the opportunity as a way of escape from the College of New Rochelle.

When asked by two of my CNR faculty colleagues, "When will you return?" I replied "Never, I hope."

---

[5] https://en.wikipedia.org/wiki/College_of_New_Rochelle

Indeed, I never returned to college teaching until twenty years later when I founded Yorktown University.

Though I left college teaching in 1980, I "stayed the course" by continuing my dedication to the recovery of classical political theory. That recovery had been occurring in Munich in Germany where Eric Voegelin in his early career was a University Professor and at Notre Dame by University of Notre Dame political theorists Gerhart Niemeyer and Eric Voegelin—a frequent Visiting Professor.

The practice of classical political philosophy, which they revived, is central to the affirmation of social order and contrary to the rationalism of the revolution in France of 1789. As such, these classical philosophers made a major contribution to ordered civil society in 20th-century America.

Unfortunately, by opposing tradition, rationalism is contributing to the death of true education, such as "character education."

Beginning in 2000, I attempted to thwart that aspect of American "higher" education by founding Yorktown University. The story of Yorktown University is told in my 2017 book, *The Coming Death and Future Resurrection of American Higher Education.*[6]

After leaving the Reagan Administration, I was asked to raise funds for Catholic friends of Count Nicolaus Lobkowicz in Eastern Europe, and though I could not speak Polish or Czech, I worked in Poland and the Czech Republic—before the collapse of the Berlin Wall.[7]

---

[6] https://www.amazon.com/Coming-Future-Resurrection-American-Education/dp/1587312743

[7] https://en.wikipedia.org/wiki/Berlin_Wall

Despite the waning influence of Communist ideology in East and Central Europe, Catholics struggled to survive the influence of lingering Russian tyranny, and Count Lobkowicz wanted to support them financially with charitable donations. He asked me to attempt a fundraising effort in America.

With the assistance of Peter Mroczk,[8] VOA's Poland director, I learned the value of the Internet by utilizing MCI Mail to communicate with Polish and Czech business managers. The state-controlled mail systems in Poland and what is now the Czech Republic would deliver my requests via Telex to meet with someone on staff who spoke English.

I learned from that experience that meetings and discussions equivalent to university classes could take place via the Internet.

University courses could be taught without classrooms!

Why build or sustain university campuses at great expense when it costs less than $2 million to found new Internet-based institutions?

The Coming Death and Future Resurrection of American Higher Education published in 2017 would not have been written but for the time I spent in Prague and Warsaw on behalf of Count Nicolaus Lobkowicz. Nor would I have gained entrée to the community of German business executives were it not for the Lobkowicz family name.

The General Partner of the Bosch Corporation whom I met in Stuttgart is one example. I remember how a guard at Bosch head-

---

[8] https://www.c-span.org/program/public-affairs-event/poland-and-solidarity/3869

quarters directed me to park at the entrance and how Bosch's managing partner Hans Merkle greeted meeting as I stepped from an elevator into his office and the rapport we established when we shared our mutual appreciation for Groucho Marx.

Not only did Dr. Merkle make a sizeable donation, but he introduced me to Henry Kissinger who agreed to give two lectures—Free of Charge!

In *The Coming Death and Future Resurrection of American Higher Education,* I describe my first meeting with Henry Kissinger in his New York office and the disconnect between the new Marriott Hotel in Prague and canned Cuban Pineapple from Castro's Cuba in store windows.

Today, college tuition is a political *hot potato* with frequent complaints about the high cost of a college degree.

In *The Coming Death and Future Resurrection of American Higher Education,* I outline thirteen ways to reform the high cost of a college diploma.

More than a decade and a half later, I can add one more way—bring a "restraint of trade action" against the Regional Accrediting Agencies—and make higher education affordable.

President Trump knows little about "Higher Education" except for the high cost of a college diploma. *The Coming Death and Future Resurrection of American Higher Education* outlines a solution.

Part Three

The 1960 Presidential election was the first Presidential election in which I was engaged practically and intellectually.

At a meeting of Young Republicans at the University of Pittsburgh at which Edward L. Flaherty, chairman of the Allegheny County Republican Party was speaker, I took advantage of Flaherty's invitation to visit him at GOP HQ by asking him to employ me. Much to my surprise, he employed me as an office boy with the Republican Executive Committee of Allegheny County. After classes at Pitt, I would go to Republican HQ and work the office switchboard.

This was an exciting experience for an 18-year-old college kid, and I enjoyed every minute of that job and the men I met, including Edward L. Flaherty, Warren Tesauro, and Cong. Bob Corbett[1] arranged employment for me in the summer of 1961 in the Office of George Gryc[2] at the General Services Administration (GSA). In November, 1960, I was privileged to stand in a line of GOP headquarters staff who greeted President Eisenhower after giving a speech endorsing the GOP Candidate for President, Richard Nixon.[3]

I was a *GS-3 Clerk Typist* at GSA and, though I was and committed to the Republican Party's philosophy of limited government, I came away from that experience at GSA with an understanding, reinforced later in my career, that government service was not for me. Yet tens of thousands of young Americans seek and obtain govern-

---

[1] https://en.wikipedia.org/wiki/Robert_J._Corbett

[2] https://www.alaskareport.com/news58/x61215_george_gryc.htm

[3] Eisenhower's speech is appended at "My Story, Part Three.

ment jobs in order to "do good" for their fellow Americans. Their "doing good" has led too often to military action aimed at spreading "Democracy."

Very soon as I focused on becoming a political scientist, I came to see that American National Government had become an instrument for "Big Government"—what we now call the "Administrative State"—which has transformed American constitutional government from one that *governed* American citizens into a "Big Government" that *ruled* its subjects.

But I get ahead of myself.

Let's start with the history of political theory[4] that I published in 1978 and which my University of Dallas colleague, Melvin Bradford, encouraged me to write.

I published The Development of Political Theory in January 1978 and only recently revisited it. Frankly, I am delighted by what I accomplished in that slim volume.

The Development of Political Theory is characteristic of all my books and essays—none is bulked out.

I can't seem to write fodder and there is none in that book.

Divided into four parts, Part One of The Development of Political Theory is a discussion of "Classical Christian Political Theory," Part Two discusses Modern Political Theory, that is followed by "Second Realities" and lastly what may be called an Epitaph to "Behaviorism."

---

[4] https://www.amazon.com/Development-Political-Theory-Critical-Analysis/dp/B003C2CKCY/

The section on "Second Realities" reflects my studies with Eric Voegelin who was in residence at Notre Dame during several semesters of my stay in graduate school at Notre Dame.

In an essay published in *VoegelinView,* Professor Linda Raeder traces the origins of Voegelin's concept of "Second Realities" to what she calls "the existential resisters" who "are dissatisfied with the lack of order they experience in personal and social existence." They manifest their dissatisfaction with reality, visible according to Raeder, in six ways:

Dissatisfaction with present existence.

· The belief that this dissatisfaction results from the intrinsically poor organization of the world. If something is not right, the reason is to be found in the evil of the world.

· The belief that salvation from the wickedness of the world is possible.

· The belief that the order of being will be changed in an historical solution, that a good world will evolve historically.

· The belief that a change in the order of being can be realized through human action, that "self-salvation" is possible through man's own effort.

· The construction of a "formula" for self- and world-salvation based upon knowledge of how to alter being.

Earlier Voegelin identified "Second Reality" constructions with ancient Gnosticism.

Part One of *The Development of Political Theory* necessarily addresses what came first in the historical development of classical Greek political theory—Anaximander, Socrates, Plato and Aristotle.

That discussion is followed in Part Two with a discussion of modern political theorists Machiavelli, Hobbes, Locke and Rousseau.

These first two parts of *The Development of Political Theory* are preceded by a discussion of cosmological myths, the break with "cosmological" symbolization of order by Anaximander and Socrates through Plato and Aristotle and my description of Christian political theory as "Philosophy of History."

All that is accomplished in 66 pages!

Of course, that brevity was a young man's mistake and I'd like to avoid a repetition here, but the best I can do is to introduce you to a fuller discussion in my 2018 essay, published in VoegelinView, titled "Conservatism and Spiritual and Social Recovery."97

Had I wanted large numbers of sales of my history of political theory, I should never have mentioned Christianity. But I can't hide the fact that my political philosophy is based in Christianity.

Rejection of Christianity is endemic to intellectual discourse in our day, however, and by stating that my approach is Christian closes many, if not all doors to professional advancement in higher education.

Fortunately, a Catholic publisher (En Route books and Media)[5] is engaged in affirmation of Christianity and will publish a 2nd edition of *The Development of Political Theory.*

After writing my Ph.D. dissertation I was attracted to teaching at the University of Dallas because Willmoore Kendall was chairman of the Department of Politics. In 1970 Kendall had published *The*

---

[5] https://enroutebooksandmedia.com

Basic Symbols of the American Political Tradition with Catholic University political theorist George Carey. But Kendall died in 1974. Upon arrival at UD, I was perceived as Kendall's replacement.

That was ridiculous, of course.

I lasted three years.

I had to make a living and was able to find employment at a Catholic woman's college, The College of New Rochelle, in New Rochelle, New York founded by the Ursuline religious order.

Quite quickly it occurred to me that just maybe I didn't belong in college level teaching, at least as an instructor, because at CNR I came into conflict with CNR's president, Sr. Dorthy Ann Kelly, OSU.

Sr. Dorothy Ann was a political and theological Liberal who bridled at the hegemony of male priests and had little appreciation for education in general and no interest in political conservatism. By opposing her intent to water down CNR's curricular standards, I earned her enmity and the respect of my faculty colleagues. When the Reagan Administration offered me a Presidential appointment in 1980, I leapt at the offer as a way of escape from CNR. When asked by my CNR colleagues "When will you return." I replied, "Never, I hope."

Indeed, I returned to college teaching in 2000 when I founded Yorktown University.[6]

---

[6] See https://www.amazon.com/Coming-Future-Resurrection-American-Education/dp/1587312743/

Eisenhower Address, Pittsburgh, November 4, 1960:

Congressman Judd, Mr. Graham, Mr. Flaherty, Senator Scott, the congressional delegation, and my fellow Americans:

After a half century in the service of the Republic, I address you tonight.

I am not here merely because of friendship for any person or out of any sense of obligation to any individual or organization of individuals. Such influences carry a great appeal but they cannot be controlling in this time of decision.

I am here solely because of my concern for the future of the United States and your hopes of peace with justice and in freedom.

That future and your deepest hopes are at stake. And they can be compressed right now to a choice between two men and their running mates.

For me, drawing on a lifetime of experience with men who want to lead and men who can lead, there is no question about the choice.

I support Richard Nixon and Henry Cabot Lodge.

In speaking to you tonight, I am sharply conscious:

Of the debt I owe this country.

Of the pride I feel as I review the long march of America, generation after generation, to leadership among the nations.

Of the hope that our grandchildren and their grandchildren will recall our days and our decisions with a like pride.

All these reasons, deep-seated in my heart, demand that I speak out on our right and duty as American citizens next Tuesday to vote-to vote our sober, serious convictions.

So doing, we shall once again justify the American faith that free men and women, voting in secret ballot, answerable only to conscience, will judge wisely as honest stewards of a grand heritage; as farsighted designers of a grand destiny.

We will not justify this faith if we are moved by selfish interest or specious promise or emotional appeal; or if we vote as members of a bloc.

The major, the over-riding, problem of today is the global struggle between those who seek to impose dictatorial domination over all men and those who seek to help all men achieve a good life in freedom.

On the outcome of this struggle depends the preservation of everything that we hold dear; the liberty that we enjoy; the opportunities we possess; the just peace we purpose.

Should we lose this struggle, Communism would darken the light of the world.

This international struggle defines the character, scope and importance of every domestic question argued and publicized in this political campaign. The primary importance of these debated issues is their effect upon our ability to win the ideological war.

To make America's world leadership felt and effective in this vast conflict, we must be strong—strong morally, economically and, indeed, militarily—as we are tonight.

Strength cannot be conjured out of glittering generalities and promises; out of fanciful pictures of a life of ease—devoid of labor, sacrifice and self-dedication; out of a grab-bag of easy answers for hard questions.

If we are to be respected and our leadership willingly accepted, the substance of our strength must be realized and felt. Every individual among us must find his greatest happiness in constructive work—work for himself, his family, his community, our Nation.

Our moral strength must never waver; never weaken before the blackmail of threat; never degenerate into surrender-infected compromise with a gun-enforced tyranny.

Our military strength must be, at whatever cost, so maintained that never again will the United States through military weakness be plunged into war—as it was three times within this century.

To fortify our economic strength, we must pay our way, not thoughtlessly piling an ever-mounting debt upon the shoulders of our children and our grandchildren and forfeiting the confidence of other nations.

We must be proud of our heritage, diligent in its maintenance and determined in its continued development; neither deserting our traditions, nor downgrading ourselves.

We must have leadership—leadership of the very finest kind that we can produce. In this campaign, only in Richard Nixon and Ambassador Lodge is the best of such leadership to be found.

I say this because they possess a rich experience in waging the kind of war in which we are now engaged; in meeting the needs of our Nation to support our world purposes; and in leading us to victory.

What I am talking about is not a matter of predicting the number of motels to be built in a given time; of forecasting to the dollar the amount of money that will be spent on gadgets and luxuries in the next four years; or of guaranteeing precisely the number of jobs that will be filled at a distant date.

The matter of which I speak—of indescribable and lasting importance to every individual among us—is the application of integrity and intellect and experience to countless problems, always directly affecting our domestic strength and our progress toward peace; they are always changing in their context and in their priorities; but always changeless in their demand for sober, resolute, steady minds.

In the campaign of our opponents, the juggling of promises by the inexperienced, the appeal to immediate gain and selfishness, the distortion of fact, the quick changes from fantastic charge to covert retreat—all these are intended to confuse the voter; not to enlighten him.

And this is nothing new. The tactics of confusion have always been a device to cover weakness in principle or in purpose or in proposal. They are still the arsenal of those who lack a constructive program founded on tested principle.

Out of the complexities Of modern living, our political opponents construct a jungle of problems which, they say, are impossible of solution except by the formulas they have dreamed up and would like to test-on us and on the world. If allowed to do so—if elected—they will call the tune, but we—and those who come after us—will pay the piper, and we will have to pay, because their announced plans call for swollen costs and mushrooming expenditures.

Now our opponents of course are experts at assuring us that neither higher taxes nor deficit spending will be used to meet these additional costs. But all history shows the absurdity of this claim.

Now this is a time for woodshed honesty—even if the American people have to apply a little woodshed discipline to get it. Unless they do, the American family will pay the costs out of its family budget because either Federal taxes will skyrocket once again or the cheap dollar and higher prices will return.

Now, of course, political opponents promise us more dollars in our pockets so that we can meet the cost of their schemes. But purchasing power at the corner grocery comes from creative and productive work, not from Federal printing presses grinding out dollars that constantly buy less—less food—less clothing—less shelter.

My friends, all gains made by labor rest on one foundation—a stable dollar. Possibly, for a time, a wage earner receiving a constantly increasing number of dollars in his pay envelope may imagine he is keeping even with the speed that his dollars cheapen. But accelerated inflation soon destroys even this poor hope and reduces it to futility.

But think of the man living on a fixed pension, or the man whose savings are in bonds and insurance policies, or the one who has nothing but his social security.

The effect on him is catastrophic.

Does this show concern for our senior citizens? A concern so prated about in some of the other platforms we read—platform planks in Los Angeles.

These wizards in fiscal shell games try to prove that all problems can be solved by bigger government, bigger spending, bigger promises. They are idolatrous worshippers of bigness—especially of big government.

But we must recognize that:

All our problems are still human problems.

All our goals are still human goals.

Therefore, for the proper conduct of human affairs, we must have:

Character that endures; not campaign promises that evaporate.

Ability that elevates; not ambition that corrupts.

Responsibility that deliberates; not rashness that stampedes.

Experience in duty that sobers; not eagerness for power that intoxicates.

Richard Nixon and Cabot Lodge, in this light, are worthy of your choice as well as mine. They have been tried and trained, tested and proved worthy.

One thought more.

Almost sixteen and a half years ago, almost on the very eve of D-Day, I became absorbed in a soul-wracking problem. A senior staff officer of mine, a tested and gallant battle leader, came to me to express his conviction that part of the plan that I had devised and approved would require the destruction of two fine American divisions—two airborne divisions of gallant soldiers. He prophesied that if I went on with this movement, these two divisions would suffer at least 90 percent casualties, even before they could land. Manifestly, if this were true, their sacrifice would be futile, because there would be no remaining strength.

If he were right, it appeared that the attack on Utah Beach was probably hopeless, and this meant that the whole operation suddenly acquired a degree of risk, even foolhardiness, that could generate a gigantic failure, possibly Allied defeat in Europe.

And the decision was squarely up to me. There was no one to help me. Professional and technical advice and counsel had been exhausted.

There was nothing for me to do but to go to my tent and think out this problem alone. I realized, of course, that if I disregarded the advice of my technical expert and trusted associate, and if his predictions should be true, then I would carry to my grave the unbearable burden of a conscience justly accusing me of indifference to the lives of thousands of Americans, and of a stupid, blind sacrifice of thousands of the flower of America's sons. Outweighing any personal burden, however, was the fact that if he were right the effect of the disaster would be far more than local; it would likely affect the entire force and probably cause a gigantic repulse on the beaches.

Now seriously I reviewed every single step in my battle plan. Having completed that study—I phoned to him and said the attack would go as stated.

Now events proved, happily, his prediction to be wrong. And I am glad to say that the first notice that came to me of the successful landing was from this same man, whose joy knew no limits.

But for years thereafter, I felt that only once in a lifetime could a problem of that sort weigh so heavily upon a man's mind and heart.

Now my fellow Americans, now that I know that in this age the President encounters soul-wracking problems many times in a single term of office, I really realize what we are asking the next President to do. This kind of problem comes to him in every conceivable form, almost every day that he is in office.

Not the fate of two divisions or even of an entire landing force but the fate of millions of Americans—young and old, military and civilian, city dwellers and farm families—the fate of the Republic itself might depend on his decision.

When the push of a button may mean obliteration of countless humans, the President of the United States must be forever on guard against any inclination on his part to impetuosity; to arrogance; to headlong action; to expediency; to facile maneuvers; even to the popularity of an action as opposed to the rightness of an action.

He cannot worry about headlines; how the next opinion poll will rate him; how his political future will be affected.

He must worry only about the good—the long-term, abiding, permanent good—of all America.

The nakedness of the battlefield when the soldier is all alone in the smoke and the clamor and the terror of war is comparable to the loneliness—at times—of the Presidency. These are the times when one man must conscientiously, deliberately, prayerfully, scrutinize every argument, every proposal, every prediction, every alternative, every probable outcome of his action and then—all alone—make his decision.

In that moment he can draw on no brain trust; no pressure group; no warehouse of trick phrases, no facile answers. Even his most trusted associates and friends cannot help him in that moment. He can draw only upon the truths and principles responsible for America's birth and development, applying them to the problem immediately before him in the light of a broad experience with men and nations.

He will be face to face with himself, his conscience, his measure of wisdom. And he will have to pray for Divine guidance from Almighty God.

And that is exactly where every thoughtful American will be, and what he should do, when he marks his secret ballot next Tuesday.

Out of that knowledge of the duties and the burdens of the Presidency, and of the responsibility of the good citizen, I must vote for Richard Nixon and Cabot Lodge November 8th.

Thank you and good night.

Part Four

After writing my Ph.D. dissertation, I was attracted to seek employment as an Assistant Professor of Politics at the University of Dallas because Willmoore Kendall was chairman of the Department.

In 1970 Kendall had published The Basic Symbols of the American Political Tradition with Catholic University political theorist George Carey. *Basic Symbols* refocuses American politics from the Declaration of Independence to its more substantial basis in Western political history starting with Cicero, St. Augustine and St. Thomas.

But Kendall died in 1974.

After several attempts by UD's President, Donald Cowan and his wife, Louise Cowan, failed to hire an established academic as Kendall's replacement, I was hired.

Apparently my colleague, Professor Melvin Bradford, had been impressed when he visited my new Faculty office in Braniff and saw an Old English dictionary on my office bookshelf. Though a distinguished Professor of Literature, Bradford appreciated my interest in Old English but Bradford was also knowledgeable about Eric Voegelin and disapproved of the Straussian emphasis on close reading of classic texts because that method tended to ignore the political, theoretical and historical truths they embodied.

As a student of Eric Voegelin I was not a *Straussians,* and Bradford had high hopes for me. But I lasted only three years, fired by Paul Eidelberg, a Straussian.

I had to make a living, of course, and was able to find employment only at a Catholic woman's college, the College of New

Rochelle, in New Rochelle, New York, founded by the Ursuline religious order.

Quite quickly it occurred to me that just maybe I didn't belong in college level teaching because at the College of New Rochelle I came into immediate conflict with CNR's president, Sr. Dorthy Ann Kelly, OSU.

Sr. Dorothy Ann was a political and theological Liberal who bridled at the hegemony of male Catholic priests, had little appreciation for education in general and had no understanding of the importance of Catholic education.

By opposing her intent to water down CNR's curricular standards in order to increase enrollments, I earned Sr. Dorothy Ann's enmity but, I also earned the respect of my faculty colleagues. When the Reagan Administration offered me a Presidential appointment in 1980, however, I leapt at the opportunity as a way of escape from CNR. When asked by two of my CNR faculty colleagues "When will you return. "I replied "Never, I hope."

Indeed, I never returned to college teaching until twenty years later when I founded Yorktown University.

Though I left college teaching in 1980, I "stayed the course" by continuing my dedication to the recovery of classical political theory. That recovery had been occurring in Munich in Germany where Eric Voegelin in his early career was a University Professor and at Notre Dame by University of Notre Dame political theorists Stanley Parry, and Gerhart Niemeyer who were joined by Eric Voegelin— a frequent Visiting Professor.

The practice of classical political philosophy which they revived is central to the conservative "rebellion" against the rationalism of the revolution in France of 1789 and a major contribution to ordered civil society in 20th century America.

Unfortunately, rationalism is infectious and is contributing to the death of true education.

In *The Conservative Rebellion,*[1] I describe why those who fought the intellectual infection of French rationalism are true *rebels.*

Beginning in 2000 I attempted to reform American "higher" education by founding Yorktown University. The story of Yorktown University is told in my 2017 book, *The Coming Death and Future Resurrection of American Higher Education.*[2]

After leaving the Reagan Administration I was asked to raise funds for Catholic friends of Count Nicolaus Lobkowicz in Eastern Europe and though I could not speak Polish or Czech, I worked in Poland and the Czech Republic—before the collapse of the Berlin Wall.[3]

Despite the waning influence of Communist ideology, Catholics in Eastern Europe struggled to survive Soviet tyranny and Count Lobkowicz wanted to support them financially with charitable donations. He asked me to attempt a fundraising effort in America.

---

[1] https://www.amazon.com/Conservative-Rebellion-Richard-Bishirjian-Ph-D/dp/1587311585/

[2] https://www.amazon.com/Coming-Future-Resurrection-American-Education/dp/1587312743/

[3] https://en.wikipedia.org/wiki/Berlin_Wall

With the assistance of Peter Mroczk,[4] VOA's Poland director, I learned the value of the Internet by utilizing MCI Mail to communicate with Polish and Czech business managers. The state controlled mail systems in Poland and what is now the Czech Republic would deliver my requests via Telex to meet with someone on staff who spoke English.

I learned from that experience that meetings and discussions equivalent to university classes could take place via the Internet.

University courses could be taught without classrooms!

To attain academic accreditation and participate in "Title IV" federal tuition assistance programs, why build and sustain university campuses at great expense when it costs less than $2 million to found and sustain new Internet-based institutions?

The Coming Death and Future Resurrection of American Higher Education published in 2017 would not have been written but for the time I spent in Prague and Warsaw on behalf of Count Nicolaus Lobkowicz. Nor would I have gained entrée to the community of German business executives were it not for the Lobkowicz family name,

The General Partner of the Bosch Corporation whom I met in Stuttgart is one example.

Not only did he make a sizeable donation, but he introduced me to Henry Kissinger who agreed to give two lectures—Free of Charge!

In *The Coming Death and Future Resurrection of American Higher Education*, I describe my first meeting with Henry Kisssinger

---

[4] Mroczyk, son of a Polish aviator and an English national, spoke accentless English.

in his New York office and the disconnect between the new Marriott Hotel in Prague and canned Cuban Pineapple from Castro's Cuba in store windows.

Today college tuition is a political *hot potato* with frequent and well-justified complaints about the high cost of a college degree.

Based on my experience working for Lobkowicz, in *The Coming Death and Future Resurrection of American Higher Education*, I discuss ways to reform the high cost of a college diploma.

1. How Tuition Debt is Hurting our College Students
2. Why American Higher Education operates as a Cartel
3. The Terrible Cost of Accreditation and U.S. Government Regulations
4. How "Regional Accreditation" Assures "Creative Destruction"
5. Why One Thousand Colleges may be Forced to Close by 2022
6. The Destructive Growth of Federal Control of Higher Education
7. The South's "Legacy of Suppression" in regulating Higher Education
8. How "Smart Money" Bought Colleges and Why They left the U.S.
9. How U.S. Secretary of Education, Margaret Spellings, destroyed the Liberal Arts
10. How Robert Shireman made For-Profit Higher Education a "Class Enemy
11. How Little it Costs to create an Internet University
12. Differences between Distance and. Classroom Learning

13. Thirteen Ways to reform American Higher Education

More than a decade and a half later in 2025 I can add one more way—bring a "restraint of trade action" against the Regional Accrediting Agencies—and make higher education affordable.

President Trump knows little about "Higher Education" except for the high cost of a college diploma. *The Coming Death and Future Resurrection of American Higher Education* outlines a solution.

Part Five

It is now the year 2026 and as I read newspapers, popular magazines, listen to National Public Radio, watch cable television, attend Catholic Mass, and commiserate with American academics teaching at deracinated institutions of "higher" Education called "Colleges" and "Universities" I am conscious that American secular culture has had at least one hundred and twenty-five years to effect a closing not only of the American mind but a closing of the soul of America.

Students of Eric Voegelin understand that inanimate objects don't have souls, but nations whose character is shaped by their past, current and future history are "ensouled."

This essay, which was first published in the now defunct journal, *Anamnesis,* examines the relationship between social recovery and how the American regime is interpreted. As such it is a fitting closure to *My Story.* Here I examine how a philosophic interpretation of the American nation's existence in history conflicts with interpretations of the American regime by reference to the Declaration of Independence.

I want to discuss the concept of "nationhood" as a mystical substance of a people's common existence because an interpretation of the American regime focused on the Declaration of Independence cannot accurately explain the phenomenon of ordered response to social disorder. By what means this nation endures in time can be understood only by philosophical analysis, not by the manipulation of Enlightenment symbols.

In *The Conservative Rebellion*,[1] I examine political periods in American history by reference to a type of "Rebel" who rose to the challenge of his times. The Colonial era in America was characterized by "rebels" who acted bravely at Lexington and Concord and is commonly known as "the Spirit of '76." In our era, if there is hope for recovery from the infection of "Liberal" ideology, that hope may be found in *daimonic* souls of men and women who by experience of the transcendent God respond to spiritual disorder by living socially effective--that is, ordered-personal lives.

Spiritual order in twentieth-century America was challenged by political ideologies that disrupted the nation states of Europe after World War I and which, in America, took the form of a political religion of democracy identified with Woodrow Wilson. That "political religion," became socially effective with the entry of the United States into World War I, continued to be effective in the political life of the United States at the end of the twentieth century and into the 21st century,

The disordered reason of Woodrow Wilson, who saw America as a secular "Christ nation,"[2] had its genesis in American "Transcendentalism" which imported German idealism into America's intellectual culture. That idealism, or "idealist humanism," saw man as essentially divine and history as the working out of the consciousness of man's divinity. Essentially anti-Christian, Transcendentalism helped heighten animosities between North and South that led to a failure to compromise and, ultimately, a Civil War.

---

[1] https://www.amazon.com/Conservative-Rebellion-Richard-Bishirjian-Ph-D/dp/1587311585

[2] See https://www.richardmgamble.com/the-war-for-righteousness

This Transcendental, *idealist* influence, combined with the publication of Darwin's *On the Origin of Species* and a Civil War that shocked Americans unprepared for massive casualties and crippling injuries, challenged the religious beliefs of combatants and civilians.

A consequence of our Civil War was the loss of belief in Protestant Christianity, and that unbelief eventually shaped the secular culture of 20th century America. In this context, it becomes clear that what we call "Conservatism" is one of several responses to spiritual disorder in American society because it offers, I believe, some small hope for recovery from disordered consciousness.

As a political theorist, if I cannot examine a people's understanding of nationhood as the mystical substance of their common existence – if my philosophy is essentially apolitical – I miss important aspects of a society's history. Nor can I examine any people's understanding of nationhood if I follow some of my fellow political theorists who neglect the historical aspects of texts that were written to address a specific political conflict, and endow those texts with meanings that are, at best, conjectural.

Let it be clear, I am the first to admit that "Conservatism" is an "ism" and a concept with which many are, and should be, uncomfortable. I prefer to use the concept, "conservative community," to describe a social reality that offers some respite from secularism, political ideology, and the many viral "isms" that infect the American body politic.

I am also aware that most, if not all, of Eric Voegelin's German students are far to my "Left" politically and, unlike American students of Voegelin, seem unaware of, nor interested in, the restorative role that political conservatives have played in the recovery of order from the effects of America's intellectual disorder. Since Voegelin's political philosophy guides my understanding of what intellectual and social forces can counter modern ideology, I need to address why Voegelin was uncomfortable with what here I am calling "conservatism."

Let me tie all this together with this observation from *The Conservative Rebellion*:

"Over time, the American people have come to understand their nationhood as the mystical substance of their common existence. How this paradigmatic reality of the life of a nation is articulated shapes the American nation for action in history."

The ancient Greek philosopher, Plato, explains in the *Republic* that men live their lives as if they lived in a cave, hidden from light, where they can only see shadows. He explains, however, that *we are forced to turn around* and ascend to the light where we may see that reality which before we saw reflected only in shadows. (514a-517a).

Philosophy is the act of *turning around* and that turning around occurs when, Plato observed, we comprehend a new truth about god: "The god is not the cause of all things, but of the good." (380c).

What we find in Plato's philosophy is a new critical insight into the relation of man to God, and the nature of divine reality.

From this theological insight we may discover important ways to interpret the American regime. What, therefore, is it that unites a people's past, its present, and the lives of those not yet born?

I will be guided by Gerhart Niemeyer's discussion of this reality in *Between Nothingness and Paradise.*[3] There he begins with the observation that the bond between political order and the order of being has been a casualty of "ideology."

Because most Americans today have lost the "faith of our fathers," we must ask "What is this bond between political and social order and being that has been lost?"

For the answer to that question we must go back to the natural philosophers of ancient Greece who discovered "being" as the origin of "nature," especially Anaximander[4], who realized that being is divine [ix].

From the beginning of philosophy's break with cosmological myth, philosophers were conscious of being (*to on*) as "mystical"— that which is beyond existing things (*ta onta*)— or what is sometimes called "nonobjective reality."

St. Augustine expresses this mystic concept of order by means of a City in this world which is not of this world; Augustine's City-- centered on Christ-- is intertwined with a City of Man lacking a divine center. Thus, the City of God has a common consciousness and experiences a common movement or peregrination of the soul that leads to an end beyond the world.

The City of Man has no end beyond this life and symbolizes the aimless social disorder of America today.

How is this related to an American nation that continues in historical time?

---

[3] https://www.amazon.com/Between-Nothingness-Paradise-Gerhart-Niemeyer/dp/0807107131/

[4] https://en.wikipedia.org/wiki/Anaximander

Unlike human beings, a society does not by its nature have a personal memory. By analogy, Niemeyer writes, a society has a remembered past by reference to "a present unity of action" that is like the "identity of a person," except society "is not a natural substance . . . [A] society . . . is lacking this tangible phenomenon testifying to identity, the past alone is what could give identity to a society."

Society is a "created" thing, not a natural person.

At the start, therefore, a society has no past, but over time materials of a historical past are created into a consciousness of a historical past.

An example that, Niemeyer observes, is ancient Israel:

"The fact is that the escapees from Egypt, when they finally stood in safety and freedom, experienced their deliverance as an act of God, an irruption of divine might into time and the affairs of men."

How different was this experience of Israel's God from the gods of other peoples of the ancient Near East?

One aspect of this difference was the awareness that the God of Israel was not a "cosmological" god.

For millennia, mankind understood that man lives in a cosmos full—or consisting of gods.

Before and with the natural philosophers, Socrates and Plato broke with cosmic consciousness of the gods of the cosmos that shaped ancient man's understanding of the origin of the world and of empires.

Ancient Israel, however, interpreted its existence by remembering a one-time intervention by God in history. Niemeyer writes:

"A cosmological myth can be celebrated by reenacting again and again the story it relates. But an event that happened once in time and

place, "before our eyes," even though experienced as a theophany, cannot be repeated or reenacted. God acted one time and his action can be only remembered."

Niemeyer writes that "once the Exodus theophany had grown into the order of a people living under God on the strength of their public past, history had become a mold of human existence, as a model not only for 'Jacob and his son' but for the entire human race."

In 1964, Voegelin thought American "conservatism" was an "ism," an ideology much like the totalitarian movements of Nazism and Fascism he experienced in Germany.

Consciousness of a public past deeply affects our present understanding, and there are some societies, such as Germany, that must confront the bad aspects of their past. Totalitarian movements in Europe after World War I left what some call a "dark past" of trauma that "cannot be assimilated or accepted."[5]

That explains the discomfort that Eric Voegelin expressed when Gerhart Niemeyer conducted an event at the Chicago meeting of the American Political Science Association (APSA) in 1964 which featured writings by Voegelin.

The experience of Voegelin and his generation of German and Austrian scholars with Nazism led to a rejection of the political movements of that traumatic past. Voegelin complained that the APSA event had "a strong slant toward conservative politics."

In this context, it is of use to consider that in modern Germany the word for "patriotic" has fallen into disuse because of the Nazi's

---

5

use of the term. The discomfort with American conservatism that many of Voegelin's German students feel is similar and explains why, I believe, so many walked away from Voegelin's first formulation of modernity as Gnostic. It was, simply, too political, for German Voegelinians escaping political reality in political theory.

Historical consciousness, however, defines the West and cannot be ignored.

Consciousness of time – past, present and future – is a condition of Western human existence.

Niemeyer writes, "Through its public past a community participates in the logos which remains the same in the flux of mutability; hence the community's identity imitates, as Boethius said, 'the ever simultaneous present immutability of God's life,' which is what one should rightly call eternal.

From this perspective, our nationhood as citizens of the United States, Niemeyer writes, "hinges on the all-important experience of a past at which a meeting occurred between time and eternity."

Consciousness of that history shapes our understanding of the life of the American nation: an understanding that can only be explained by myth.

Though it may seem improbable that the identity of modern America is shaped by myths, Niemeyer lists a number of truths we Americans affirm that are true myths, including:

- We believe that individuals have souls;
- We proclaim an essential personal dignity and independence of mind;
- We distinguish time from eternity;

- We attribute authority to "the people" and to the "law";
- We affirm an enduring Constitution; and
- We affirm that we as a nation exist "under God."

These myths do not depend on the consent of every American to their truth. Niemeyer suggests that the carriers of the truths of our myths may even be concentrated in a "remnant."

This recalls what Aristotle explained about *right by nature.*

What is right can be known by mature men, he said, and often we know it by reference to someone who knows what is right.

In life, we often ask ourselves, "What would he do?" That he or she may be someone we know who can be relied upon for good advice. This is a powerful force in our private and in our public lives.

There are persons who guide others in ways that can be political, moral, or simply "just." The reality of their presence in our lives is celebrated in art, literature, and film. For that reason, education from elementary to secondary school through college should aim to grow good character and replenish the numbers of mature, daimonic, men and women in each generation.

Niemeyer takes this essentially Aristotelian formulation and sharpens it with the assertion that:

"Christianity is the center of our culture, the truth that has shaped our past and is still shaping our present, regardless of what the attitude of particular persons to it may be. We cannot realistically step out of this truth into "another one," we cannot in truth become Hindus or Buddhists, and least of all can an amalgam be made of all religions as a dwelling place for anybody."

"Western civilization came into existence through the unifying impulse of Latin Christianity. No other religion has ever wielded a similarly powerful influence in the centuries of our cultural identity. The historical metamorphoses of our culture can be understood only in their relations to the Christian origins, even where these metamorphoses have not worked for but rather against Christianity."

At this late stage in the decline of the West, it is unlikely that the Western Christianity can be recovered.

As Christianity ceases to be a living experience in the West, the historical consciousness central to the nature of Western nations will be diluted. There is no modern Clovis to convert to Christianity and the ancient tribes of Western Europe have consolidated into modern, secular nation-states.

No modern religious based "Great Awakening" is likely to occur today, nor would it have lasting consequences were it to occur.

But there are restorative forces at work in every historical society, such as ancient Israel and Greece, the Christian West and Confucian China.

Eric Voegelin writes, "The man who lives in the erotic tension to his ground of being is called *daimonios aner*, i.e., a man who consciously exists in the tension of the in-between (*metaxy*), in which the divine and the human partake of each other."

Aristotle's equivalent for the *daimonios aner* is the *spoudaios*, sometimes translated "mature man."

Christian theology speaks of the reality of living in a State of Grace. I think the concept "daimonic" explains not only Socrate's daimon but also the response of our American souls to order in the face of today's disorders. We should not overlook, therefore, the presence of *daimonic* men and women who daily contend against the forces of corrosion of civil society by ideological movements. These men and women are essential for renewal, for reducing the influence of political ideology in American life, and for recovery from cultural disorders.

That many such daimonic men are political "conservatives" suggests that American conservatives are playing a role in correcting the disorders that afflict our times.

Americans are "doers" not original "thinkers" thus the response to disorder by American conservatives has had greater influence in actions, rather than in theories. Interpretation of these actions then shapes how we interpret the American regime. If we interpret the American revolution and the Constitutional order established solely in light of the "Enlightenment" ideals displayed in the Declaration of Independence, we lose sight of the essential aspects of nationhood as the mystical substance of our common existence and the response of daimonic men and women to that source of order and the ideological disorders of their times.

The visible signs of a vibrant recovery of order in 2025 can be found in the actions of many American political conservatives when, over time, they respond to social disorder.

Consider the response of Presidents Harding and Coolidge to the excesses and economic consequences of Woodrow Wilson's entry of the United States in World War I.

Consider the response of Taft conservatives to labor violence in the late 1940s, of Ronald Reagan's response to the Soviet Union, or response of conservatives to the 1973 decision in the U.S. Supreme Court in *Roe v. Wade*, inspiring the "Right to Life" movement.

Cultural conditions that foster good character are fragile, however, so we must ask, at the end of the 21st century will there be a vibrant, powerful, and spiritually healthy American nation?

Will we even remember the civilization of the Christian West?

Or will we suffer a loss of history and learn to accept bad economics, bad religion, failures in imperial foreign policy, and the uncertainty of a world of forces seeking to destroy our country?

Just as Plato saw that the best regime must affirm a new truth about God, all this will occur, if we interpret the American nation by reference solely to the Declaration of Independence and not by reference to a philosophy that affirms our nation's participation in the divine ground and the force for good of daimonic men.

Notes

[i] Richard Bishirjian. "Leo Strauss and the American Political Religion." *Modern Age*, Vol. 56, No. 4 (Fall, 2014).

[2] This discussion is based on and is an expansion of my discussion in "VI, Daimonic Men and 'Recovery,'" in *The Conservative Rebellion* (St. Augustine's Press, 2015), 154–63.

[3] See my discussion of modern ideologies in chapter 10 of my *Development of Political Theory: A Critical Analysis*, with H. Lee Cheek, 2006.

[4] See Richard Gamble. "Savior Nation: Wilson and the Gospel of Service." *Humanitas*, Vol. XIV, No. 1 p. 7.

[5] See Thomas Fleming, *A Disease in the Public Mind* (Boston: Da Capo, 2014).

[6] Ideological interpretations of the Declaration of Independence that ignore the history of the document, how it was authorized, and variations in the three drafts of the Declaration make possible an argument that the Declaration, not the Constitution, is the basis of the American regime. This is the analysis of Robert Kagan, who asserts that "the Declaration of Independence was at once an assertion of this radical principle, a justification for rebellion, and the founding document of American nationhood." *Dangerous Nation: America's Foreign Policy From Its Earliest Days to the Dawn of the Twentieth Century.* (New York: Vintage Books, 2006) p. 40-41.

[7] Bishirjian, *Conservative Rebellion*, 2.

[8] Plato, The Republic of Plato, Allan Bloom trans. (New York: Basic Books, 1968), p. 58.

[9] For an authoritative discussion of this discovery by Anaximander see Werner Jaeger. *The Theology of the Early Greek Philosophers.* (New York: Oxford Univ., 1967) pp. 24-37.

[10] Gerhart Niemeyer. *Between Nothingness and Paradise.* (Baton Rouge, LA: Louisiana State University, 1971) p. 145

[11] Ibid., 155.

[12] Ibid., 160.

[13] Ibid., 162.

[14] Anthony Polonsky and Joanna B. Michlic, eds., *The Neighbors Respond: The Controversy over the Jedwabne Massacre in Poland* (Princeton: Princeton University Press, 2004), 2.

[15] *The Collected Works of Eric Voegelin*, ed. Thomas Hollweck, vol. 30, *Selected Correspondence: 1950–1984* (Colombia: University of Missouri Press, 2007), 472.

[16] Eric Voegelin, The New Science of Politics. An Introduction. (Chicago: University of Chicago Press, 1952).

[17] Niemeyer, *Between Nothingness and Paradise*, 177–78.

[18] Niemeyer, *Between Nothingness and Paradise*, 174.

[19] Ibid., 191.

[20] Ibid., 193.

[21] Aristotle, *Nicomachean Ethics*, trans. Martin Ostwald (Indianapolis: Bobbs-Merrill, 1962). "Thus, what is good and pleasant differs with different characteristics or conditions, and perhaps the chief distinction of a man of high moral standards is his ability to see the truth in each particular moral question, since he is, as it were, the standard and measure for such questions" (1113a24). See also 1166a10, 1176a15, and 1176b20.

[22] Gerhart Niemeyer, "Christian Studies and the Liberal Arts College," in *The Loss and Recovery of Truth* (South Bend, IN: St. Augustine's Press, 2013), 511.

[23] Eric Voegelin, *Anamnesis*, Gerhrat Niemeyer trans. (Notre Dame, IN: University of Notre Dame Press, 1978), 154.

[24] Aristotle, *Nicomachean Ethics*, 1094a 19–26.

Part Six

My Story would not be complete if I did not mention "modern Gnosticism."

Walter A. McDougall's *Promised Land, Crusader State: The American Encounter with the World Since 1776*[1] examines the aspiration to control nature on display in Jeff Bezos'[2] and Richard Branson's[3] plans for rocket flights into space.

The desire, even the will, to control nature underlies 21st century space exploration much as the Renaissance Hermeticists used "magic" to achieve that control.

In sum, Jeff Bezos and Richard Branson reveal a very strong arrogance that permeates American culture.

Like Bezos who launched his "Blue Origin" rocket from a field in Texas and Branson launched "Virgin Galactic's" commercial vehicle for space tourism, we must add a third: Elon Musk's[4]"SpaceX."

Musk's "SpaceX" is designed to enable humanity to become a space-based civilization. Unfortunately, Musk's concern about the future of mankind reveals the disturbed mind of a *modern* man unhindered by theology, philosophy or a sense of human limits.

---

[1] https://www.amazon.com/Promised-Land-Crusader-State-Encounter/dp/0395901324/

[2] https://en.wikipedia.org/wiki/Jeff_Bezos

[3] https://www.biography.com/business-leaders/richard-branson

[4] See https://bishirjian.substack.com/p/three-modern-gnostics

Musk was preceded by thinkers similarly motivated to control nature.

The Renaissance Hermeticists developed a view of magic as a means to predict the future and control nature. You can read about them in Frances Yates' study of Giordano Bruno[5] or in my essay titled "*Modern Political Religion*"[6] published at VoegelinView.com.

The history of Renaissance magic is part of a long tradition of attempts to free us from our humanity in the false realization that we are gods.

We are not gods, of course, and we see in Musk, Bezos and Branson a glimpse of those Renaissance magicians who aspired to transcend our mortality in gnostic speculative knowledge that we are gods.

Modern Gnosticism much like the Gnostics of 2nd century AD claims to have special or "secret" knowledge.

The intellectual culture of the *philosophes*, what Alexis de Tocqueville called *esprit revolutionaire*, is what political theorists today understand is a form of "political religion."

The term "political religion" might strike some as unacceptable. On the one hand, those who piously affirm the tenets of orthodox spiritual traditions and attest to the reality of their faith may resent the suggestion that modern intellectual and mass movements can be analyzed on the level of religious experience.

On the other hand, ideologists whose claims appear in the guise of "scientific" judgments will reject the suggestion that their political

---

[5] https://www.amazon.com/Giordano-Bruno-Hermetic-Tradition-Frances/dp/0226950077/

[6] https://voegelinview.com/modern-political-religion/

views are religious in nature. They distinguish between their own "rational" principles and the "irrational" beliefs of those who proclaim the truth of religion. Even adherents of some churches maintain that their creeds are not rational but are wholly based on suprarational "religious" truth. We must add, however, that there are "religions" other than those which articulate a belief in God.

There is no lack of scholarship which has identified the religious character of certain political movements. Albert Camus in *The Rebel* (1951) analyzes the variants of rebellion in modern speculation and the spiritual character of revolt.[7] Norman Cohn's *The Pursuit of the Millennium* (1957),[8] an analysis of medieval European religious movements which is perhaps best known, shows the similarity of these movements to the modern political phenomena of German National Socialism and Communism. These contemporary political ideologies, Cohn shows, are similar in structure to—and in some instances take inspiration from—what we today would call the fanatical, if not irrational, medieval phenomena.

L. Talmon's *The Origins of Totalitarian Democracy* (1960)[9] indicates the similarity of the secular apocalyptic strain in eighteenth century French philosophy to the chiliastic medieval phenomena. He also traces the revolutionary consequences of this political Messianism in eighteenth century France. Robert Tucker's *Philosophy*

---

[7] https://www.amazon.com/Rebel-Essay-Man-Revolt/dp/0679733841

[8] https://www.amazon.com/Pursuit-Millennium-Revolutionary-Millenarians-Anarchists/dp/0195004566/

[9] https://www.amazon.com/Origins-Totalitarian-Democracy-Hardcover/dp/9356983283/

and Myth in Karl Marx (1961)[10] persuasively shows the origins of the thought of Karl Marx in the revolution in religion instituted by Idealist philosophy's creation of an image of man as God.

But perhaps most important for analysis of the nature of modern political religions are the works of Eric Voegelin in which he argued in *The New Science of Politics* (1952)[11] and *Science, Politics and Gnosticism* (1959)[12] that these political movements are similar to beliefs of the ancient Gnostics. More recently, Daniel P. Walker and Frances Yates have shown the influence of Renaissance Hermeticism in the formation of modern political thought. Collectively we can follow Voegelin's use of Robert Musil and characterize the thought of the *philosophes*, the German idealists and the later thought of Karl Marx as modern "Second Realities."

The concept of another, or "Second Reality," following Robert Musil, explains the ideological attempts to replace reality with another, more acceptable reality originating in the mind of modern ideologists.

Rejection of reality, a characteristic of modern intellectuals, was not always predominant. The ancient Greek philosopher, Aristotle, for example, explored the consubstantiality of human *nous* (mind or spirit) with a divine *nous* and saw that man actualizes his humanity in the aspiration to be "deathless" through noetic contemplation of

---

[10] https://www.amazon.com/Philosophy-Myth-Karl-Robert-Tucker/dp/0765806444/

[11] https://www.amazon.com/New-Science-Politics-Introduction-Foundation/dp/0226861147

[12] https://www.amazon.com/Science-Politics-Gnosticism-Essays-Paperback/dp/0895264196/

the divine. Man realizes his humanity in contemplation of the divine, not rejection of divine reality.

This consciousness of the opening of the soul to transcendent *nous* in Greek philosophy was an event in history of Western consciousness.

No longer could the compact experience of being within the medium of the cosmological myths define intellectual culture. A new consciousness of transcendence of the divine beyond existence and essence was experienced by Greek natural philosophers as an historical development.

That insight into the historical dimension of existence as a process in time was first formulated by Anaximander:

"The origin (arche) of things is the Apeiron . . . . It is necessary for things to perish into that from which they were born; for they pay one another penalty for their injustice (adikia) according to the ordinance of Time."

Anaximander experienced existence as a creaturely process which is perishable but nevertheless consubstantial with a timeless Apeiron or "boundless" condition that is begun to be seen as the origin of the process of existence. Thus Anaximander observes, "it is necessary for things to perish," an acknowledgment, on the one hand, of the reality of death, and, and on the other, of the reality of immortality since what exists will "perish into that from which they were born," which is to say that they will return to the divine *arche* of being.

Eric Voegelin writes of this fragment of Anaximander:

"Reality was experienced by Anaximander . . . as a cosmic process in which things emerge from, and disappear into, the nonexistence of

the Apeiron. Things do not exist out of themselves, all at once and forever; they exist out of the ground to which they return. Hence, to exist means to participate in two modes of reality: (1) In the Apeiron as the timeless arche of things and (2) In the ordered succession of things as the manifestation of the Apeiron in time."

The mystery of reality as a process of participation in the divine origin of being was experienced by the ancient Greek and Christian philosophers as a process pointing ultimately towards transfiguration of reality.

Plato's concept, displayed in the Myth of the Cave, of the turning around of the *psyche* towards the transcendent Good beyond existence and essence in his *Republic* and St. Augustine's concept of the peregrination of the city of God and the souls of men towards Christ articulate this experience.

The ascent *(epanodos) of* the soul to the Agathon in Platonic philosophy, just as the conversion of the soul to God of the Christian experience, articulates a transformation of the soul. Yet this experience did not occlude a simultaneous creaturely experience of the *psyche* in the world. Body which is ensouled is also *psyche* which is embodied. Physical, creaturely existence is reality.

In the Gnostic movement of antiquity in which the scattered diffusion of the divine spark ends in a pneumatic process of running back to the godhead, however, this "balance of consciousness," to use Eric Voegelin's concept, is lost.

The creaturely world is rejected as is the humanity of man.

Experience of existence as a mode of participation is occluded by absolute identification with the divine. The Gnostic experience of the divine, hidden God, from which the Gnostic adept was an emanation, left no room for the noetic experience of the participative nature of human consciousness, of the goodness of the cosmos and of material existence.

It left only the transfiguring experience of gnosis.

In 1952, Eric Voegelin, attracted by the similarity of ancient Gnosticism to modern political religions, extended the typology of ancient Gnosticism to an analysis of contemporary political ideologies in order to delimit the religious experience which engendered them. Modern Gnosticism, he found:

"may be primarily intellectual and assume the form of speculative penetration of the mystery of creation and existence, as, for instance, in the contemplative gnosis of Hegel or Schelling. Or it may be primarily emotional and assume the human soul, as, for instance, in paracletic sectarian leaders. Or it may be primarily volitional and assume the form of activist redemption of man and society, as in the instance of revolutionary activists like Comte, Marx, or Hitler. These Gnostic experiences, in the amplitude of their variety, are the core of the redivinization of society, for the men who fall into these experiences divinize themselves by substituting more massive modes of participation in divinity for faith in the Christian sense."

This modern Gnostic "redivinization of society" is itself a transvaluation of the Christian "dedivinization" of the temporal sphere which was the outcome of the clash between Christianity and pagan culture and its gods. Christian apologists "dedivinized" man and society by expelling the gods from the world. They thus reordered the Western interpretation of man's existence "through the experience of man's destination, by the grace of the world-transcendent God, toward eternal life in beatific vision."

A "dedivinization" could not have occurred without the experiential atrophy of polytheism and its challenge in the form of the Christian experience. Thus identification of the contemporary "redivinization" of modern Gnosticism presupposes the atrophy of the Christian experience in intellectual culture and its replacement by a religious experience which is impatient with the uncertainties and anxieties, the insecurity, which accompanies a world without gods. Eric Voegelin explains this as follows:

". . .when the world is de-divinized, communication with the world-transcendent God is reduced to the tenuous bond of faith, in the sense of Heb. 11:1, as the substance of things hoped for and the proof of things unseen. Ontologically, the substance of things hoped for is. nowhere to be found but in faith itself; and, epistemologically, there is no proof for things unseen but again this very faith. The bond is tenuous, indeed, and it may snap easily. The life of the soul in openness toward God, the waiting, the periods of aridity and dullness, guilt and despondency, contrition and repentance, forsakenness and hope against hope, the silent stirrings of love and grace, trembling on the verge of a certainty which if gained is loss-the very lightness of this fabric may prove too heavy a burden for men who lust for massively possessive experience."

Two aspects of the Gnostic derailment, first. occlusion of creaturely existence and second, absolute identification of "man" with God by the Gnostics, became formative elements in the shaping of modern political religion.

This is important for understanding the effects in America of the brutality of the American Civil War, Darwin's *Origins of the Species* and the role of American Transcendentalists in bringing German idealism to the United States. The development and transmission of the ideas of philosophic idealism in Germany began with Renaissance Hermeticism

Renaissance Hermeticism

Despite the finding in 1614 by the philologist Isaac Casaubon[13] (1559-1614) that the Hermetic writings of Hermes Trismegistus were in fact post-Christian in origin, fanatic devotees of Hermeticism rejected the evidence. Committed to the reform of religion by an infusion of the thought of Hermes, the new Renaissance messiahs were not deflected from their redemptive paths by a scholarly argument that the documents on which their new religion was based were not what they believed them to be. The thought of Hermes Trismegistus, though little known to us today, was believed by Renaissance scholars to constitute an ancient revelation predating the revelation of Moses and the philosophy of the ancient Greeks.

Marsilio Ficino

Renaissance Neo-Platonists like Marsilio Ficino (1433-1499) attempted to revive the *prisca theologia* (antique theology) of Hermes and reconcile it with Christianity. Later, persons like Giordano Bruno would abandon this Christian interpretation and simply assert the truth of Hermeticism. That was the natural outgrowth of a radical and philosophical testament.

---

[13] https://en.wikipedia.org/wiki/Isaac_Casaubon

The central focus of ancient Hermeticism was the belief that Hermes saw that the human *nous* is itself divine. Those who attain to this knowledge are saved by becoming God. The core of Renaissance Hermeticism was a radical deification of man, with similar anthropological consequences.

The ideas that Marsilio Ficino are representative. Ficino wrote of the existence of the "divine mind" in men, living, shining, and reflecting itself there. By that Ficino meant that man is the image of God in the sense that his true being is a reflection of the "divine face" or divine goodness. God, he wrote, in willing himself, "wills all other things which are God Himself as being in God, and as flowing out of God are images of the divine face and have as their end the task of reproducing and confirming the divine goodness. "

The symbol of the "flowing out" or emanation of existent things in God breaks the distinction of kind between creaturely existence and the divine and alter it to a difference of degree. Consequently, Ficino could write that if God is goodness, then the soul becomes God by love of goodness. "Just as, not he who sees the good, but he who wills it becomes good, so the Soul becomes divine. not from considering God, but from loving Him." Ficino writes also:

"The entire effort of our Soul is to become God. This effort is as natural to man as that of flying is to birds. For it is inherent in all men, everywhere and always; therefore it does not follow the incidental quality of some man, but the nature of the species itself."

Giovanni Pico della Mirandola

The Renaissance nobleman, Giovanni Pico della Mirandola[14] also expressed these ideas in his "Oration on the Dignity of Man," first published as part of a proposed disputation to defend 900 theses on religion, philosophy, natural philosophy, and magic. Though the concept of the "dignity of man" has been absorbed into orthodox Catholic understanding of man's nature, this short oration is a virtual compendium of the Hermetic deification of man.

Unfortunately, the disputation which was to occur in Rome in January 1487 never took place because an alert Pope Innocent VIII, suspecting the heretical cast of some of Giovanni Pico's theses, prohibited the disputation and ordered an investigation. The somewhat restricted Christian Hermeticism of Ficino and Giovanni Pico gave place in the late sixteenth century to the aggressive revival of Hermetic *prisca theologia* by Giordano Bruno.

Giordano Bruno[15]

Bruno was accused of saying that he intended to "found a new sect under the name of philosophy," a form of competition frowned upon by the Inquisitors who burned him at the stake in 1600. Bruno viewed himself as a Messiah come to save the world through a renaissance of Hermetic magic. In his *Spaccio della bestia trionfante*

---

[14] https://en.wikipedia.org/wiki/Giovanni_Pico_della_Mirandola

[15] https://en.wikipedia.org/wiki/Giordano_Bruno

(1584), Bruno openly advocates the making of "familiar, affable and domestic gods" as the means of world renewal.

In that work, Jupiter admonishes the other gods to reform themselves, promising that "if we thus renew our heaven, the constellations and influences shall be new, the impressions and fortunes shall be new, for all things depend on this upper world . . . ." The magician participates in this celestial renewal by divinations which evoke the good traits of the gods and thus simultaneously reduce the influence of their bad traits. This attitude conflicts with the ancient Gnostic antipathy to the material world, but the Hermetic corpus also contained the basically non-Gnostic religious view of the world as a manifestation of God.

This acceptance of the world in a transfigured state, but not in its present reality, was a principal formative element in the view of nature of Idealist Humanism. In one aspect of the *Corpus Hermeticum,* for example, the world is viewed as transparent to a world spirit or God which itself images forth the "greater god." All beings in the world are by that token in God.

In the "Lament" of the Hermetic *Asclepius,* the view of imminent decline is coupled with the view of world reform. In the old age of the world, evil, as opposed to good, will prevail, the gods will depart from man, and the order of nature will collapse. But this condition is not final. At some point in this decline, God will intervene by means of a flood or consuming fire that will destroy evil, and the world will be returned to its original beauty. "That is what the rebirth of the world will be; a renewal of all good things, a holy and most solemn restoration of Nature herself, imposed by force in the course of time. . .by the will of God."

Perhaps persuaded that culture was undergoing a process of renewal, the Renaissance Magus found this Hermetic view quite appealing since he viewed his own action to be somehow participating in a greater process of world renewal. Underlying Renaissance Hermeticism is a subtle change from the Medieval understanding of man. What has changed is Man, now no longer only the pious spectator of God's wonders in the creation, and worshipper of God himself above the creation, but Man the operator, Man who seeks to draw power from the divine and natural order.

This view was spread widely. Frances Yates and Paul Kristeller see the immediate influence of the Hermeticism of Ficino and Bruno in "Galileo's claim that man's knowledge of mathematics is different in quantity but not in kind from that of God Himself"; in the natural magic of Shakespeare's plays; the political theory and action of Campanella; the growth of Rosicrucianism and Freemasonry; Sir Thomas Moore's critique of Cartesian naturalism; and Francis Bacon's *New Atlantis*[16] [25].

German Idealism

And though the atheist humanism of Karl Marx has had a lasting impact on the lives of communist regimes, in the United States, a more subtle influence of German idealism can be found in their influence on American Transcendentalists whose belief in man as god led to a political religion of democracy.

---

[16] https://en.wikipedia.org/wiki/New_Atlantis

Fredrich Schiller[17]

Fredrich Schiller's (1759 –1805) lecture, "The Nature and Value of Universal History," given at Jena near Weimar, Germany is an example. In that lecture Schiller attempts to replace the reality of the depth of the human with the substitute depth of universal history. Classically trained, German idealists understood that the "depth" was a philosophic symbol of Heraclitus of Ephesus.

A fragment of Heraclitus reads as follows:
You would not find the boundaries of soul
even by travelling along every path,
so deep is the logos it has.

Schiller's lecture is revealing because he admits that the depth of universal history, which he substitutes for the depth of the soul, is an "optical illusion."[26] Though an optical illusion, it is necessary because through the conjecture of an illusion enables the philosopher of universal history to become the immortal "Lord of History."

Schiller was not alone in engaging in such speculation. Robert Tucker argues that the origin of German Idealism as an identifiable ideological movement may be found in Immanuel Kant's (1724 – 1804) "expression of a compulsion in man to achieve absolute moral self-perfection."[27]

---

[17] https://en.wikipedia.org/wiki/Friedrich_Schiller

Immanuel Kant[18]

Immanuel Kant saw man's will as his "proper" or real self, and this he called the "divine man within us." Kant wrote in the *Groundwork of the Metaphysic of Morals* that our ideal will which makes universal laws is the proper object of reverence. In other words, Kant viewed man as godlike and moral action as an attempt to harmonize our own will with that of God's, even though such harmony cannot be attained by finite beings.

Johann Fichte[19]

Johann Gottlieb Fichte (1724 –1804) added to this intellectual development by portraying history in terms of the "Divine Idea" or the life of God. The scholar who by his intellect lives in the Divine Idea, embodies it and his whole thought is engrossed in the thought of the Idea. His existence is a thought of God. Robert Tucker calls this "the displacement of God by the godlike self." The difference of kind between man and God is now seen by German idealists as a mere difference of degree. For the Idealist enterprise to succeed, the distinction between man and God must be cast aside and replaced with a man-god. In Fichte's mind "history"–understood as the movement of being–is moving toward a this-worldly resolution of contradictions in existence.

---

[18] https://en.wikipedia.org/wiki/Immanuel_Kant

[19] https://en.wikipedia.org/wiki/Johann_Gottlieb_Fichte

Millennialism

This expectation, that historical reality was moving toward transformation–a this worldly millennium–is sometimes called "Millenarian." Though in its specific sense this concept refers to that period one thousand years in advance of the final judgment of man when the saints rule with Christ in a kingdom established in this world, the term is often more broadly construed to define historical movements called "chiliastic." A Greek word referring to the millennium.

A specific definition of these movements was made by Norman Cohn, the great historian and author of "Pursuit of the Millennium," who identifies five aspects of political movements seeking this-worldly salvation. They are:

(1) collective, in the sense that it is to be enjoyed by the faithful as a group;
(2) terrestrial, in the sense that it is to be realized on this earth and not in some otherworldly heaven;
(3) imminent, in the sense that it is to come both soon and suddenly;
(4) total, in the sense that it is utterly to transform life on earth, so that the new dispensation will be no mere improvement on the present but perfection itself;
(5) accomplished by agencies which are consciously regarded as supernatural. [28]

Historical representative of these movements are the *pauperes* of the first Crusade, who saw the rescue of Jerusalem as the culmination of the eschatological movement that would result in the establishment of the "New Jerusalem" of the Book of Revelation; the Flagellants, who indulged in self-mutilation which they believed would hasten the establishment of the millennium; and the radical Taborites.

American Transcendentalists

In America, millennial chiliasts saw divine significance in the American Revolution and the American Civil War, out of which they expected would be forged an America committed to the redemption of the world. Some of the key influences in this development were Julia Ward Howe, author of the *Battle Hymn of the Republic*, Samuel Gridley Howe, her husband Theodore Parker, the influential Unitarian minister, and Ralph Waldo Emerson.

Emerson's "Concord Hymn," is an attempt to interpret the American revolution as the beginning of the redemption of the world by a democratic America.

> By the rude bridge that arched the flood,
> Their flag to April's breeze unfurled,
> Here once the embattled farmers stood
> And fired the shot heard round the world.

That "shot" was heard in Boston, not "round the world.

The epitome of eschatological hopes for America was evoked in Julia Ward Howe's "The Battle Hymn of the Republic," published in February, 1862.

The Battle Hymn is a poetic, though secularized, rendition of the millennial passages of the Book of Revelation where the "glory of the coming of the Lord;" the "trampling out the vintage where the grapes of wrath are stored" (which in the manuscript version more closely approximates the scriptural language, "He is trampling out the wine press . . ."), the personal testimony of the chiliast who attests that she has "seen Him" in the bloody events of the American Civil War and who announces that she can "read a fiery gospel writ in burnished rows of steel."

Julia Howe transforms Christ's redemptive mission–which is not of this world–into the world immanent social activism of the Anti-Slavery movement: "With a glory in his bosom that transfigures you and me: As he died to make men holy, let us die to make men free. . . ."[29]

Theodore Parker and many New England Transcendentalists were enthusiastic about the Hungarian patriot, Lajos Kossuth, who opposed the Habsburgs and sought to unite east central Europe in a loose federation. And their ideas fueled the Anti-Slavery movement with a political religion that deflected compromise.

Development of a political religion of democracy in America was extremely important. We may see that in this observation by Irving Kristol.

". . . once upon a time, in this country the question of democracy was a matter for political philosophy rather than for faith. And the way in which a democratic political philosophy was gradually and

inexorably transformed into a democratic faith seems to me to be perhaps the most important problem in American intellectual–and ultimately political history."[30]

Two persons who represent such a transition and who left a deep impression on early twentieth century American intellectual culture, were Herbert Croly and Woodrow Wilson.

Herbert Croly

Herbert Croly's *The Promise of American Life* (1909) and later the journal, *The New Republic,* which he founded and edited, performed a role in shaping the political attitudes of America's intellectual elite in the Progressive era, a role which Woodrow Wilson complemented by shaping the popular attitudes of Americans towards democracy, the nature of peace, and America's destiny.

In *The Promise of American Life*, Croly wrote: "For better or worse, democracy cannot be disentangled from an aspiration toward human perfectibility, and hence from the adoption of measures looking in the direction of realizing such an aspiration." That aspiration would be realized primarily, he thought, by those "exceptional fellow countrymen" of his, the American intellectuals whom he called "saints." These secular saints who lead the common mass, Croly speculated, will not necessarily be conservators of the American political tradition.

The realization of the promise of American life will sometimes require a "partial renunciation" of the American past and of present interests, if necessary to contribute to the "national purpose." There may even occur a sudden transfiguration by "an outburst of enthusiasm." He observed:

"If such a moment ever arrives, it will be partly the creation of some democratic evangelist-some imitator of Jesus who will reveal to men the path whereby they may enter into spiritual possession of their individual and social achievements, and immeasurably increase them by virtue of personal regeneration."

Let us reassemble the parts of Herbert Croly's political religion before examining the political religion of Woodrow Wilson.

Woodrow Wilson

Dominating Woodrow Wilson's civil religion are four aspects:

First, the view of a national purpose to be realized in public affairs. Second, is the realization that this purpose requires secular saints, themselves led by a messiah who will reveal the true path. Third, Croly sees this as a transfiguration that will come because the American nation itself is formed by a democratic ideal which is working its way in time towards full realization. Fourth, before this can occur, this democratic ideal, always a promise, must he fully articulated, its creed formulated now, so that the American people may believe once again in the promise of American life.

A critique of Croly's civil religion requires that we return to basics. Politics is a science of four principles:1) rational judgments informed by an awareness of circumstances, 2) a proper assessment of the limits of government and potential abuses of state power, 3) a concern for institutions which limit power, and 4) prudent knowledge of the common good. Croly's call for secular saints who will conduct us into a condition of reconstituted and transfigured reality, has less to do with political science than with prophecy, enthusiasm, and magic.

The national life is indeed informed by an idea, by public myths which articulate the commonly shared beliefs of society's members. But that idea does not exist independently nor is it working its way in human events towards a logical fulfillment. The national life can expire, change its form, become something altogether different, not by means of the twists and turns of a world spirit, but by the weakening or collapse of civic virtue and of political judgment. How swiftly such a collapse can occur, and how vulnerable the American political system is to such collapse, is visible in the influence of Woodrow Wilson's political religion.

Informing Wilson's political religion is a view of history similar to Croly's. History, Wilson believed, moves according to a plan in which America plays a major role. His view of history is one of a progressive development, moving slowly but inexorably to a condition of reconstituted reality. In an address in Pittsburgh, Pennsylvania at a Y.M.C.A. celebration on October 24, 1914, he said:

"*. . . no man can look at the past of the history of this world without seeing a vision of the future of the history of this world; and when you think of the accumulated moral forces that have made one age better than another age in the progress of mankind, then you can open your eyes to the vision. You can see that age by age, though with a blind struggle in the dust of the road, though often mistaking the path and losing its way in the mire, mankind is yet-sometimes with bloody hands and battered knees-nevertheless struggling step after step up the slow stages to the day when he shall live in the full light which shines* *upon the uplands, where all the light that illumines mankind shines direct from the face of God."*[31]

The role of America in this plan of history, Wilson was persuaded, was shaped and directed by God from the beginning. This, he declared on one occasion, is a nation God built with our hands.

To what end, we might ask?

In an address before Confederate veterans of the Civil War on June 5, 1917, Wilson declared that "we are to be an instrument in the hands of God to see that liberty is made secure for mankind." Wilson's view of history in which America and mankind were moving to a world- immanent transfiguration of the human condition was not an isolated facet of the thought of an otherwise pragmatic man of affairs. Instead, it was an integral aspect of his attitude towards life and the skills required, if political life was to be governed rightly.

Politics, for Wilson, required "vision," and vision for Wilson meant knowledge of God's purpose in history. In his First Inaugural, Wilson was speaking of his own visionary politics when he described his task as "no mere task of politics." Politics of Woodrow Wilson was not mere politics, politics was a special capacity to announce the immanence of a new age certified by the political leader who experienced a special revelation.

Woodrow Wilson's vision of America was one of a nation ordained to play a mighty role in history; it was only fitting, therefore, that Americans should be perceived as different from the rest of the peoples of the world. We, for example, entered World War I "for no selfish advantage." Our troops were "the armies of God." Accordingly, America undertook missions of redemption.

At St. Louis, Missouri, September 5, 1919, Wilson observed that:

"(America) . . . has said to mankind at her birth: "We have come to redeem the world by giving it liberty and justice." Now we are called upon before the tribunal of mankind to redeem that immortal pledge."

Wilson was an idealist in the sense that T.H. Green[32] defined an idealist as one who seeks to "enact God in the world" by the pursuit of ideals not given in experience. Wilson was committed to the ideal of a world absent of war, a world he believed to be within the grasp of a civilized world. And America's entry into World War I was largely motivated by the desire to attain such an ideal. That it was to be accomplished by violence did not dismay Wilson.

It is important to understand that Wilson's desire to involve us in World War I was grounded in his will to destroy the system of balance-of-power politics. Wilson's oft repeated assertion that America had no selfish interest to be satisfied by her entry into the war, that we sought no territory, no concessions, was his way of expressing utter contempt for balance-of-power politics.

On July 10, 1919, in his address to the United States Senate presenting the treaty of peace with Germany, Wilson proclaimed:

"Every true heart in the world, and every enlightened judgment demanded that, at whatever cost of independent action, every government that took thought for its people or for justice or for ordered freedom would lend itself to a new purpose and utterly destroy the old order of international politics."

Wilson's desire to "utterly destroy" the reality of balance of powers was yoked with his desire to destroy "autocratic authority." He was persuaded that only governments governed by majority rule, not by autocratic minorities, could truly seek peace. As a consequence, he sought to destroy autocratic governments, in the present instance, the government of Kaiser Wilhelm. In such a "good cause" Wilson believed that the maximum use of force was acceptable. Wilson saw a "halo" around the musket over the mantle of the citizen soldier who fought to redeem the world, and around the returning American troops. Force, apparently, was not to be disdained when executed by the "armies of God."

Wilson was in search of a "cause" in which to destroy the existing world order and found it in "the terrible war for democracy and human rights."

That war was "terrible" no doubt in part because the winners of the conflict, "the only people in the world who are going to reap the harvest of the future are the people who can entertain ideals, who can follow ideals to the death." But the war would be "terrible" also because Woodrow Wilson saw the war in apocalyptic terms. For Woodrow Wilson this war had eschatological significance.

Wilson called the war a "final contest" which would bring about a "final emancipation." And if America did not join the League of Nations, he foresaw another "final war"; for surely there would be war again, he said, one that would bring the evil policies of the powers of this world to a close.

By looking at history as a progressive movement towards a transfigured condition of peace and justice, Wilson saw himself as living in the last days when heroic acts were necessary to bring history to fruition.

Notes:

[1] See Joseph Epstein, *Alexis De Tocqueville, Democracy's Guide* (New York, Harper Collins, Eminent Lives, 2006).

[2] Originally published as *Wissenschaft, Politik and Gnosis* (Munich: Kosel-Verlag, 1959), English edition, William J. Fitzpatrick, trans. *Science, Politics and Gnosticism. Two Essays.* Chicago: Henry Refinery Co., Gateway Edition, 1968).

[3] Eric Voegelin, "On Debate and Existence," *Intercollegiate Review, III* (1967), 143-152.

[4] Quoted in Voegelin, *The Ecumenic Age,* 174.

[5] *Ibid.* Throughout this section our interpretation has relied on Voegelin's analysis of what he calls the "Balance of Consciousness," *The Ecumenic Age,* Chapter Four, Section 3, 227-238.

[6] Plato, *The Republic,* 529c.

[7] Eric Voegelin, *The New Science of Politics* (Chicago: University of Chicago Press, 1952), 124.

[8] *Ibid., 107.*

[9] That atrophy occurred after the American Civil War.

[10] *Ibid.*, 122.

[11] See Richard Gamble, The *Battle Hymn of the Republic* and American Civil Religion (Fall 2014), Vol. 56, No. 4.

[12] Jonas, *The Gnostic Religion,* 149.

[13] *Ibid.*, 79.

[14] *Ibid., 145.*

[15] *Ibid., 264.*

[16] *Ibid., 269.*

[17] *Ibid., 337.*

[18] A translation of Giovanni Pico's "Oration" is available in E. Cassirer, P.O. Kristeller, J.H. Randall, Jr., eds. *The Renaissance Philosophy of Man* (Chicago: University of Chicago Press, 1948), 223-254.

[19] Frances Yates, *Giordano Bruno and the Hermetic Tradition (Chicago: University of Chicago Press, 1964), 212.*

[20] Yates, *Giordano Bruno, 218.*

[21] *Ibid., 221-222.*

[22] *Ibid., 33.*

[23] *Ibid., 39-40.*

[24] *Ibid., 144.*

[25] Paul Oskar Kristeller, Renaissance *Concepts of ' Man and Other Essays (New York: Harper Torchbooks, Harper and Row, Publishers, 1972), 20; Yates, Giordano Bruno, 357; 360-397; 413; 274; 427;" 450.*

[26] See Eric Voegelin, "The Eclipse of Reality," in *The Collected Works, Vol. 28*, eds. Thomas Hollweck and Paul Caringella (Baton Rouge, 1989: Louisiana State University Press, 1989), p. 122-139).

[27] Robert Tucker, *Philosophy and Myth in Karl Marx* (Cambridge: At the University Press, 1965), p. 33.

[28] Norman Cohn, "Medieval Millenarism: Its Bearing on the Comparative Study of Millenarian Movements," in Sylvia L. Thrupp, ed., *Millennial Dreams in Action* (New York: Schocken Books, 1970), 31.

[29] Ernest Lee Tuveson, *Redeemer Nation. The Idea of America's Millennial Role* (Chicago: University of Chicago Press, 1968), 197-198.

[30] Irving Kristol, *On the Democratic Idea in America* (New York: Harper & Row, 1972), p. 51.

[31] All citations of Wilson's speeches may be accessed from the "E-Library Search" at the website of The Woodrow Wilson Presidential Library and Museum http://www.woodrowwilson.org/ library-archives/wilson-elibrary

[32] Richard Bishirjian, "Thomas Hill Green's Political Philosophy," in *The Political Science Reviewer*, Vol. 4 (Fall 1974), pp. 29-53.

About the Author

Richard J. Bishirjian was Founding President and Professor of Government at Yorktown University from 2000-2016. He earned a B.A. from the University of Pittsburgh (1964) and a Ph.D. in Government and International Studies from the University of Notre Dame (1971).

Bishirjian, a native of Pittsburgh, Pennsylvania, was active in the William Pitt Debate Union and the Society for Conservative Studies at the University of Pittsburgh.

Dr. Bishirjian taught at universities and colleges in Indiana, Texas, and New York.

He is the editor of *A Public Philosophy Reader (1978)* and *The Development of Political Theory* (1978) and the author of five recent scholarly books and a political novel.

- Book: Ennobling Encounters, En Route Books, 2021.
- Novel: "Coda," En Route Books 2021.
- Book: Rise and Fall of the American Empire, En Route Books 2021.
- Book: Conscience and Power, En Route Books 2021.
- Book: The Coming Death and Future Resurrection of American Higher Education, St. Augustine Publishers, 2017.
- Book: The Conservative Rebellion, St. Augustine Publishers, 2015
- A new edition of Bishirjian's *Development of Political Theory (1978)* will be published by En Route Books in 2025.

- Dr. Bishirjian publishes daily reflections at Substack. (https://bishirjian.substack.com).

www.ingramcontent.com/pod-product-compliance
Lightning Source LLC
LaVergne TN
LVHW040221110826
845146LV00005B/1366

* 9 7 9 8 8 8 8 7 0 3 5 9 5 *